The Reading Teacher's Handbook

JO PHENIX

Pembroke Publishers Limited

© 2002 Folens Limited

Pembroke Publishers
538 Hood Road
Markham, Ontario, Canada L3R 3K9
www.pembrokepublishers.com

Distributed in the U.S. by Stenhouse Publishers
477 Congress Street
Portland, ME 04101
www.stenhouse.com

This edition is adapted from a book written by Jo Phenix and first published by Folens Limited (UK).
E-mail: folens@folens.com

National Library of Canada Cataloguing in Publication Data

Phenix, Jo
    The reading teacher's handbook/Jo Phenix

Includes index.
ISBN 1-55138-145-1

    1. Reading (Elementary) I. Title.

LB1573.P47 2002   372.4   C2002-902916-3

Editor: Carol-Ann Freeman
Layout artist: Patricia Hollingsworth, Jay Tee Graphics
Illustrations: Andrew Noble
Cover Design: John Zehethofer

Printed and bound in Canada
9 8 7 6 5 4 3 2 1

Contents

Chapter 1

Understanding the reading process

The way we teach reading reflects our understanding of the reading process, and our beliefs about which skills are important. Reading is far more complicated than sounding out words, or trying to remember them all. It is a complex thinking process in which a reader uses many different kinds of cues in order to get meaning. We make predictions about meaning based on our knowledge of the subject and on what we have read so far. We predict words by our knowledge of the syntactic patterns of language. We confirm our predictions by looking at as much of the phonic and graphic information as we need. Reading is not a matter of choosing one of these cueing systems to focus on, either as a reader or as a teacher. A fluent reader is one who can use all cues in varying degrees as each individual reading task demands. Instead of choosing a methodology and sticking with it, we must develop a repertoire of techniques to teach children how to access the meanings in print, reflect on these meanings and respond appropriately.

Our most important resource for teaching reading is real books; books children will want to read for fun and for information. Some of these books should be written in the language of children, and should deal with the everyday events that make up their lives. This will give them easy access to meaning and help them develop confidence as readers. Other books should represent the best of language and storytelling, both classical and new. These will help children

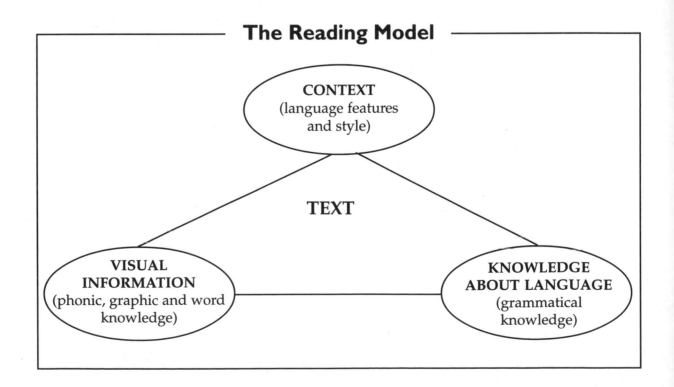

The Reading Model

CONTEXT
(language features
and style)

TEXT

VISUAL
INFORMATION
(phonic, graphic and word
knowledge)

KNOWLEDGE
ABOUT LANGUAGE
(grammatical
knowledge)

develop a love of reading, and refine and expand their uses of and appreciation for language and literature. The classroom should also contain books written by the children. As well as having its own intrinsic value, writing is one of the best ways for children to learn about language, and access the language of others.

Regular reading of a variety of materials is a prerequisite for becoming a proficient and enthusiastic reader. However, quantity reading is not enough to ensure that all children will reach their potential as readers. There are times when we need to step into the process, to focus the children's thinking, broaden their experience, teach specific skills, demonstrate what fluent readers do and help the children read more effectively.

That is what this book is about. It is a collection of ideas, strategies and hands-on activities for teaching reading. The activities can be used before, during and after a reading session and include talking, writing, drama and visual arts. When teachers add their own ideas, interests and talents, the result can be a classroom full of purposeful and interesting activities that will engage children in language, and set children on the road to becoming lifelong readers.

Reading skills

If we are to teach reading successfully, we must understand the skills involved. By 'skills' we mean what children need to know to be successful at a reading task.

Research indicates that there are predominantly three kinds of information that enable a reader to understand the meaning of a text: context, language and visual information. We use these three cues simultaneously and in varying degrees as we read.

Helping children to use context

Context is concerned with meaning and prior knowledge. We use context as we read by calling on our prior knowledge of the subject matter to form expectations and make predictions about the meaning. The more we know about the subject before we read, the better we will comprehend what we read. If we understand what we are reading, we will also know when we make a mistake and will reread to correct our miscue.

Children are most likely to use context cues effectively when they are engaged by the content of the text. When their reading material is relevant to their lives they can draw on their prior knowledge to help comprehension. When the content of their reading matches their interests, they will see purpose and relevance in reading.

Key points

✔ Draw the children's attention to examples of print and text serving a particular purpose in the world around and outside the classroom. Help them to notice signs, labels, the print on television and texts with a specific purpose, for example local street names or the school noticeboard.

✔ Set the context of the text before studying it: "This is a fairy story which used to be told to young children."; "This book should help us to find more information about the Arctic."; "I found this report in last night's newspaper."

✔ Set some questions which the children must try to answer as they read. What type of book is it? What is its purpose? Who is it intended for? Does it have particular features? How well does this text do its job?

✔ Choose material that is likely to match the children's prior knowledge. They will then be able to draw on their own experience to help them to understand and at least some of the vocabulary will be familiar to them.

✔ Use a 'shared' approach to introduce the children to material which is above their independent reading levels. Use a wide range of both fiction and non-fiction for different purposes and audiences. Select at least some material which has been written for 'real' situations, for example a recipe book, instruction manual, comics, diary and so on.

✔ Make sure children know that their goal is to understand, enjoy or gain information from the book. Discuss the content before reading to help them to predict what to expect.

✔ Before reading, provide an opportunity for the children to share or brainstorm ideas about the content and situations in the text. Try in your own discussion to use and explain any new or unfamiliar vocabulary or terminology.

✔ Teach children to recognize the main features and style of different types of text and the context in which they are likely to read them.

✔ Discuss your own strategies for reading. Do you begin at the beginning, read through the contents page or index, survey the illustrations or skim and scan to find a particular piece of information? Explain the features: chapter headings, captions and labels, diagrams, information in specific paragraphs, language style and tense and so on.

✔ Read with the children to help them through difficult constructions, sentence structure or vocabulary. Encourage them to join in, emphasizing what they can read rather than what they can't. Praise the attempts.

✔ Discuss and summarize what they have read, suggesting further reading or research. Stress that talking about what they are reading is a good way of helping them to understand.

✔ Talk about the authors and illustrators of texts and the people who help to publish them. It often helps children to know that books are written by real people. Select favorite authors and writers of non-fiction and build up collected lists of their work. Encourage the children to share examples of favorite texts: eye-catching advertisements where print is used effectively; gripping stories; amusing poetry; excellent sources of information and so on.

Helping children to use language cues

Familiarity with the patterns of grammar and syntax – the order of words in a sentence; what language is supposed to sound like – will enable us to predict what kind of word to expect in reading. It will also indicate when we have made a mistake, because what we have read will not sound like an English sentence and we will reread to correct our miscue.

Be aware of the children's own speech patterns. The more familiar children are with correct patterns of speech, the more likely they are to notice if their reading does not follow these patterns. If children's speech patterns are not grammatical (in terms of Standard English), either through inexperience or dialect differences, you may need to work on their oral language first. Let them see what their speech looks like written down and emphasize that this is written 'spoken' language by using, for example, speech bubbles.

Key points

✔ For beginning readers, choose material with repeated sentence patterns.

✔ Draw out examples of these repeated sentences in shared sessions, writing them out and encouraging the children to copy your example:

This elephant is big.

This _____ is big.

✔ Help the children by translating their normal speech patterns into written language patterns, for example "It's a tree." – "Yes! This is a tree. Now! What is this? This is a ...". Help them from the familiar to the unfamiliar by positive encouragement.

✔ Use the phrase, "Did that sound right to you?" when children make syntactic miscues. Then encourage them to reread in order to "Make it sound right."

✔ Work with the children to use literary patterns for their own writing. They may do this already, for example when they begin a story with "Once upon a time". The children can use a sentence pattern from a story or poem and substitute their own words and ideas. In this way, they will repeat sentence patterns many times and thus become more familiar with them.

✔ Children who are not native English speakers may not be able to recognize when they read ungrammatically. A certain level of familiarity with English is necessary for reading success. Focus on texts with strong patterns, such as rhymes and repeated sentence patterns.

✔ Ask children about what they have read so that they begin to recognize that understanding is as important as accuracy.

Helping children to use phonic and word recognition skills

Phonics and word recognition skills concern the actual print on the page. A glance at a word will show us how long the word is. Knowledge of how letters are used in combination to represent sounds and build words will help us to decode and identify words in the text. Other visual elements will also help in reading; for example, a word starting with a capital letter within a sentence is likely to be the name of a person or place; quotation marks indicate that someone is talking. Words that have a special relevance for the children such as 'ice cream' or 'toilets' become instantly recognizable. Context, as well as frequency of use, will enable children to recognize common service words such as *was* and *the* and they will gradually build up a sight vocabulary.

Key points

✔ An awareness of meanings and language will let us know when we have made a mistake, and will help us to make an educated prediction when words are not easy to 'sound out'.

✔ Choose reading material with strong rhythm and rhyme patterns. This will encourage children to predict words before they actually try to read them. Sometimes, read aloud a rhyming poem and pause for the children to fill in the rhyming words.

✔ Clapping or marking time to very strong rhythmic or rhyming text can help children to develop the idea of 'beats' in words as a precursor to understanding syllables.

✔ Encourage students to spell phonetically as they begin to write. Provide opportunities for frequent writing sessions. This will give children opportunities to listen for sounds and match them with letters, and will also give children their best opportunity for prolonged and purposeful practice in using phonics to construct words. Awareness of how letter sounds are used in words will enable children to decode words more successfully in their reading.

✔ Help children to 'sound out' words during shared reading sessions. Give prompts, for example "It starts like your name" or "It rhymes with heat". This will help children to make generalizations about groups of letters and the sounds they represent. Use independent sessions for children to play word games with a partner.

✔ Teach children to recognize syllables and to sound out words syllable by syllable. This will help them to decode longer words.

✔ Teach children to combine phonic information with other cues. They may be able to sound out a prefix, then use context to work out the rest of a word. Draw their attention to 'tricky bits', for example 'mother' not 'muther'.

✔ Encourage the children to try and praise reasonable or logical attempts even when not completely correct.

✔ Plan separate phonics and high-frequency word learning as structured programs to go alongside general reading and writing practice. Praise children when they use a practised word or sound correctly in their unaided writing.

Chapter 2

Organizing the reading environment

A range of activities

We know that there is wide variety in the experience, language background, ability and learning styles of the children we teach. The best way to meet these different needs, in a large class, is by providing many ways for children to interact with and respond to the texts they read.

You may find it helpful to develop your repertoire of strategies in the four categories dealt with in this book:

✔ Preparing for reading – activities to do before the reading starts.
✔ Reading – ways to access the text.
✔ Developing comprehension – activities to do after the reading.
✔ Developing skills – specific instruction in language skills.

Each of these four will apply whether the organization involves shared work, whole class work, guided group work or independent work. Many activities work well for all types of organization, but some are more appropriate to one specific type.

Grouping

Provide opportunities for children to interact with one another in many different group sizes and settings. With large and small groups you can engage the children's interest, give instruction, stimulate thought and model the thought processes of a fluent reader. When they work individually, the children will have a chance to put into practice the skills they are learning. Different groupings will also give you an opportunity to observe the children at work and note their involvement, contributions, frustrations and level of success. It is important to familiarize children, from the start, with the idea that they will not always work with the same group. Changing your groups frequently will eliminate the 'low group syndrome', in which children lower their performance to match perceived lower expectations.

Whole class

The children may work as a whole class for activities such as these:

- ✔ Modelling and demonstrating how the whole text should be interpreted.
- ✔ Focusing on a particular aspect: plot, character, setting and so on.
- ✔ Introducing a new aspect of word, sentence or text level work.
- ✔ Initial learning of skills.
- ✔ Sharing experiences and ideas before reading.
- ✔ Discussing aspects of a text after reading.
- ✔ Choral reading/readers' theatre.
- ✔ Sharing work with one another.
- ✔ Holding a debate.
- ✔ Brainstorming ideas.
- ✔ Responding through drama or role playing.
- ✔ Relating strategies and skills learned in the literacy lesson to other aspects of the curriculum.
- ✔ Applying what has been learned to new situations.

Your role in this whole class time is to engage children in the task, provide leadership and guidance, model the process of reading and stimulate reflection and response to the reading.

Small groups

You can form small groups in several ways, depending on your purpose. It is important that children do not stay in permanent groups that designate their place in the class hierarchy. Groups should be flexible and change constantly according to the planned activity.

Interest groups

The children choose an activity and work with others who have made the same choice. This might be a certain aspect of a research topic, a particular story or a follow-up activity.

Instructional groups

You can group children according to a particular skill they need to learn and provide instruction for that group.

Ability groups

You may sometimes choose to group children according to their reading ability. This does not mean that children should be relegated to 'the low group' on a permanent basis. It does mean that you can provide different kinds of help, for example:

✔ Stimulate and motivate – children who are not always successful readers are often reluctant readers.
✔ Provide suitable texts that are within the children's ability.
✔ Work with a particular group that is not able to read independently.
✔ Provide a listening tape for the group to listen to and read along with.
✔ Use guided reading techniques to set purposes for reading, limit the task and monitor progress.
✔ Provide extra challenges for more able children.

Mixed ability groups

It is often productive to group children with others of greater or lesser ability or knowledge. In this way, the group is more likely to have individuals who can assume a leadership role, take notes quickly, understand the task, and contribute ideas and language. Children who do not have the confidence to participate in large groups may be more willing to speak up in a small group. Those children who seem to be only passive observers will still be participating in the group process, making discoveries along with the others and sharing in the group's accomplishments.

However you form your groups, they can engage in a number of activities:

✔ Reinforcing skills and strategies covered in the whole class section.
✔ Moving towards independence.
✔ Reading a text in parts; discussing a text after reading; sharing ideas and information; listening to someone read aloud.
✔ Problem-solving.
✔ Planning.
✔ Preparing and listening to book talks.
✔ Word and language study.
✔ Specific skill instruction.

Your role in the group process is to motivate, while making sure groups understand and adhere to the task, providing specific help where needed. In some cases, you will work with the group to give instruction and at other times they will work as a group with another adult or work on their own without teacher support.

Guided group work

Guided work can take place in short but regular spots of about 10–15 minutes where the rest of the class is engaged in activities which do not need direct support. Once you have established the necessary routines, you will find guided group work very fruitful in terms of the learning which takes place. Sometimes guided work may be enabled if and when other adults are available.

The approach in guided work is to act as mentor, supporting the children through reading tasks in a positive way, doing everything possible to ensure success. Less able children may go over ground introduced through the shared session in a more measured way. Alternatively, the aim may be to prepare them for whole class sessions to come, ensuring that they can play a fuller role in these. Guided group work will also allow you to insert steps in skills work which may not be needed by the more able. Above all, guided work enables the group access to closer and more directed attention than they may receive from the whole class sessions.

Independent work

It is important to make a distinction between individual and independent work. In many cases, children may be working collaboratively without direct teacher or adult support. This often provides an opportunity for them to try out something independently which has been demonstrated in a whole class – shared or guided – group session. The instruction to them may be, "Now, try this as a group without my help." Repeating an activity from the shared or guided session allows them to gain confidence and to rehearse skills and strategies modelled by you.

As well as whole class and group work, children need time to work alone or in pairs. Paired work is sometimes neglected as a form of classroom organization. By encouraging children to work with a partner, you can help them develop the habit of remaining on task even when you are not there to give direct guidance. Children in pairs can discuss work more quietly than if they were in larger groups. Also, dividing a class into pairs allows for a greater range of differentiation.

Pairs and individuals can work on activities such as these:

- ✔ Independent reading.
- ✔ Follow-up activities.
- ✔ Skills activities and practice.
- ✔ Research.
- ✔ Selecting books.
- ✔ Listening to tapes.
- ✔ Journal writing.

Your role in independent work is to make sure that children know what they are to do and stick to the task. You can also talk to each child to give specific help and guidance and assess competence and progress.

The purposes of whole class, group and independent activities

Why work as a class?

✔ To give a block of new learning or knowledge to everyone at once.
✔ To pool the collective knowledge of the class.
✔ To stimulate, motivate and add new impetus and encouragement.
✔ To allow children to learn from each other.
✔ To spread ideas from a few to the whole.
✔ To provide an overview of what different sections of the class are working on.
✔ To involve everyone and allow less able children to offer ideas alongside more able.
✔ To make it easier for you to regulate, control and organize.
✔ To draw the threads of group and individual work together.
✔ To give children a chance to report back, or to give work a new direction.
✔ To provide time for discussion and reflection.
✔ To provide an opportunity to praise children who have worked hard.
✔ To give a shy or retiring child a chance to shine.
✔ To provide a 'formal' audience.

Why work in groups?

✔ To allow for differentiation by task or by outcome.
✔ To provide greater guidance in strategies and skills.
✔ To reinforce knowledge or strategies in a more supportive way.
✔ To allow you to focus on particular skills or children.
✔ To allow you to have closer and more personal involvement with the children.
✔ To enable you to try out strategies and skills in a 'safe' situation before working with the full class.
✔ To reinforce strategies and skills as necessary after the whole class session.
✔ To share resources and enable every child to use them.
✔ To allow children to work with classmates other than their usual friends or partners.
✔ To allow you to observe and monitor strategies and progress more closely.

Why provide independent activities?

✔ To allow a child to work one-to-one with you or a supporter.
✔ To give extra time to an individual.
✔ To allow for greater differentiation than can be provided within a group.
✔ To allow children to explore personal goals, preferences or ideas.
✔ To give particular children a longer time with resources.
✔ To allow children the opportunity to work away from your scrutiny.
✔ To give you more opportunity for detailed observation and monitoring.
✔ To make a diagnostic assessment.
✔ To allow you to fill gaps in records.
✔ To allow children time to collect their thoughts and ideas before or after working as part of a group.

Preparing for reading

Prior knowledge is one of the most important components in reading comprehension. In order to read with understanding, we need prior knowledge about such things as: the subject matter of the piece; the genre; the style of writing; the dialect; the meaning of the words; and punctuation marks. The more we know about these, the more predictable the reading will become; the more predictable a text is, the more fluent and meaningful our reading will be. If we do not have sufficient prior knowledge of one or several of these points, then there is likely to be little comprehension.

We can help children to activate and increase their prior knowledge of a text by preparing them for the reading task. Pre-reading activities can help them to recall and share their own experience and we can add to their knowledge about the topic, genre, vocabulary and theme.

Children also need a real purpose for reading. They need to know what the text holds, what kind of information or entertainment to expect and how it relates to their individual needs and interests. If we can stimulate their interest before they read, they will be motivated to seek out the meanings in the text.

Children who do not see themselves as fluent readers also need confidence to approach a text. The more we can prepare them for the reading task, the more success they are likely to have, and nothing breeds confidence like success.

Selecting reading material

Teachers are now becoming very familiar with the practice of using enlarged texts (big books) as sample texts for shared whole class and group work and sets of books for guided work, but there are other means of providing texts for both shared and guided work:

✔ Specially selected extracts from literature, poetry or non-fictional material.
✔ Enlarged samples of posters, leaflets and advertising material.
✔ Newspaper articles.
✔ Newspapers in education packs.
✔ Overhead transparencies.
✔ Black/white boards (electronic or not) and flip-charts.
✔ TV/camcorder links – good for demonstrating practical crafts, such as: letter formation, spelling, sentence-building and following instructions.

(Please remember to make sure that you adhere to copyright regulations in relation to the examples given above.)

Pre-reading activities

1. Glance through the pages

Read the title

Titles often signal the kind of reading that children need to do. 'The Castle Street Mystery' suggests a different kind of reading than 'How to Train Your Dog' or 'A Picture History of Stamps'. Help the children to form expectations based on the title and the book cover.

Sample questions

✔ What does the title suggest to you?

✔ Is it a sports story, mystery, adventure?

✔ Have you read this kind of story before?

Look at the author's name

Children soon begin to develop favorites among authors and this can help them to know what to expect from a text. Being aware of authors' names can also help them with book selection in the library.

Sample questions

✔ Have you read anything else by this author?

✔ What kind of writing, story and characters might you expect?

Look at the book's features

Children need to learn to distinguish between fiction and non-fiction books at an early stage since they demand different reading strategies. A book with a contents page, index and glossary will have a different purpose from one solely with chapter headings.

Children should also begin to look for a series title, front and back cover 'blurb' and other information.

Sample questions

✔ What kind of book is this?

✔ Is it likely to be fiction or non-fiction?

✔ What might we expect to find in it?

✔ What features are there to help us?

Look at the format of the pages

Different kinds of writing will involve different kinds of page layout. Recognizing a recipe, a poem or an index can let us know whether it is best to: start at the beginning and read sequentially; use alphabetical order to find the part we need to read; read silently or out loud; read only once or expect to reread, and so on. Each of these types may well have different features on the page.

Sample questions

✔ How is the print organized?

✔ Is this a story, a poem, a comic strip, a newspaper article, a map?

✔ What do you know about this kind of writing?

✔ Is there a lot of dialogue?

✔ Are there chapter headings or side headings?

✔ Are there diagrams, charts, maps, captions?

✔ What are the sub-topics?

Look at any illustrations

Talking about a picture can give you an opportunity to use vocabulary from the selection, and to talk about the mood, the setting and events. This will help the children to set expectations and predict difficult words and unfamiliar vocabulary. Some children may become over-reliant on the pictures of fiction books and still totally ignore the illustrative material in non-fiction. They need specific instruction in how these can assist the reader. Children also need to be taught about creating images of the book in their own minds. This is not as automatic as many experienced readers think.

Sample questions

✔ What is the style of illustration?
Watercolor, pencil drawing, photographic, cartoon, impressionist?

✔ Who are the characters?
People, animals, monsters, machines, aliens?

✔ What are they doing?
Do they look funny, pleasant, friendly, dangerous, afraid?

✔ Where is the setting?
City or country? Tropical, arctic, jungle, desert, ocean, outer space?
Specific location? School, pool, beach, hospital, train?
Specific event? Party, contest, accident?

✔ What is the time frame?
Past, present or future?

✔ What is the mood?
Does it look funny, mysterious, scary, magical?

✔ What is the theme?
Sports, journey, natural disaster, nature, escape?

2. Recall and share experiences

Encourage the children to share any experience or knowledge they have concerning the topic or situation they are going to read about. This is a good opportunity for children to share any expertise they may have through hobbies and interests, or tell personal anecdotes. You can prompt these recollections with questions to the group, and the children can respond in a group discussion or through writing.

Sample questions

✔ Have you ever been on a train journey?

✔ Which comic strips do you read?

✔ Can you remember ever being lost?

✔ What was the best party you have ever attended?

✔ What do you know about dolphins?

3. Formulate questions

With the children, hypothesize about the selection and help them to set expectations regarding what they are about to read. This will help them to establish a context, and also give them something specific to read for. They can just ask the questions, or write them down for later discussion.

Sample questions

✔ What problems might there be with a new puppy in the house?

✔ How do you think the children might have got stuck in the cave?

✔ What do you hope to find out about building a tree house?

✔ What do you think we might learn from this book?

4. Brainstorm ideas

Brainstorming is calling out or listing any ideas you have on a given subject without stopping to evaluate their relevance or importance at the time. It is free association. Even if an idea is not of value, it often sparks a related idea from someone else. You can ask children to brainstorm on a theme title, a story title, what is suggested by a picture, a name, an object, anything that will get them thinking of ideas related to the text they are going to read. As the children call out their ideas they will be using vocabulary related to the topic, bringing past experiences to the front of their minds and listening to other ideas; it is another way of sharing thoughts. Children can do this in small groups, with one recording the ideas as quickly as possible. For those who are not able to record fast enough, you or a volunteer can take their place. Children can sometimes follow up their initial brainstorming by categorizing, prioritizing, selecting, evaluating and sharing their ideas.

---

5. Use the book's features to help to plan and organize ideas

The **chapter headings** or **contents list** will often provide strong clues either to the plot or the sequence in which information is organized. Reading these through with the children can help to prepare them for what is to come.

A **glossary** often contains the most difficult words or technical terms. If these are read and understood in advance of the whole text, children may avoid failure.

Asking children to compile their own glossary after reading is also a good way of checking whether they have understood what they have read. You might organize a 'tit-for-tat' activity in which children select, say, ten words from the text that you must define. In return, you select ten words which the children must define.

Index

The **index** of a book can be used to help children to organize a brainstorming session into a concept map. Ask the children to select words that they can read from the index and then ask them why they think they have been included in the book. For example, if the children select the word 'krill' from the index of a book about whales, ask what they think the connection is. Having established that 'krill' is food, they could look for other food words. Then, you might select the term 'echolocation', asking the children again to speculate on the connection. Not only does this establish that the children can read the words they are likely to meet, it removes the random nature of brainstorming. Since any word in the index is going to be covered within the book, it also ensures that any questions posed by the children will be answered in the book.

You could also introduce the children to a book's blurb. Children love the name 'blurb' since it sounds like slang. Particularly for less confident children, the blurb provides advance notice of what to expect from the book. Educational publishers are increasingly including blurb and also author biographies, either on the back or inside the back cover of books, aimed at children. Children often skip this vital information in their haste to move on to the next book of a series. Since it often provides a summary of the book it can provide a taster for the book itself.

---

6. Sample the text

Read aloud a small sample of the text, or ask the children to read it for themselves. It might be the opening paragraph, or any section from the story. Afterwards, the children can: make predictions; form hypotheses; formulate questions; or perhaps do some research before proceeding.

Sample questions

✔ What kinds of problems do you think the characters might encounter?

✔ In what ways do you think this problem could be solved? Work in your group to come up with two or three possible solutions.

✔ What questions would you like to ask the author at this point? (At the end of the reading, see if these questions have been answered.)

Introduction

This book is your guide to bone-chilling frights,
the horrors revealed when you turn out the lights.
From A–Z, these tales tall and true
Will horrify and fascinate you.

Creatures who stalk on the darkest of nights,
Decaying corpses and other delights,
Graveyards with skeletons, once buried deep,
Will haunt your dreams and spoil your sleep.

Reader, beware of the terrors ahead,
The open coffins, the walking dead.
Werewolves and vampires all take a look,
At the person so brave as to open this book!

From: Virginia King, *A–Z of Horror* (Folens: Momentum Reading Scheme, 1999)

Chapter 4

Reading the selection

In order to learn what is expected of a reader, to increase fluency and to participate in the comprehension activities, each child needs first to access the text. However good a methodology is, the same one is not likely to be equally successful with every child. Different learning styles, differing abilities and different texts require a variety of approaches. One way to give each child the best chance of success is to use as many approaches as possible. This has the added benefit of bringing variety and interest to reading sessions. The following have been grouped under the headings of listening, predictable reading, guided reading, reading out loud and independent reading. The shared activities are those felt most appropriate for whole class organization, although many will prove just as valuable as guided activities with groups. Afterwards, all the children can share equally in follow-up activities that require them to process information from the text.

Having a variety of ways to read a text will give the children multi-level access to classroom reading. In many cases, children with different levels of ability will be able to share in reading and responding to the same texts. This can help to eliminate the 'low group syndrome', a condition often experienced by children who are placed in a special group for slow readers. This can cause them to lose confidence and see themselves as poor readers.

Listening

The biggest part of reading comprehension is not accessing the print, but thinking about and applying the meanings. Children who are not fluent readers, or are even non-readers, can practise all the comprehension skills as they listen to a story being read aloud.

For some children, listening is a good introduction to reading a text as they may then have enough prior knowledge of vocabulary, style and content to read the selection for themselves.

These are some ways to provide listening experiences:

✔ You can read a text aloud. Sometimes read part of the text before discussing it to make sure that the children understand what they have heard so far. Help the children to raise questions and form hypotheses about what might follow. The children may continue the same text in the guided session.
✔ Read a short extract from a story, not necessarily from the beginning. If the story can be interrupted at a 'cliff-hanger', the children will be motivated to continue later.
✔ A child or small group can rehearse and present a text to the class. This provides not only a listening experience, but also a real purpose for oral reading.

✔ Record the story on tape and play part of it during the shared session, making it available for anyone who would like to listen. Even fluent readers can gain a lot by listening to another interpretation of a text.

✔ Invite guest readers into the classroom, such as parents, other teachers or older children. Hearing another voice will bring variety to your reading class.

✔ Build up a resource of people with different dialects and language backgrounds who can read stories for you, either personally or on tape. An ethnic or regional tale becomes more real when read in its own accent or dialect.

✔ Use oral storytellers, including those who tell their story in another dialect. Here again, the children are freed from the restraints of decoding and can observe such things as gestures, movement, mime and pitch. If desired, the story might then be reproduced on tape or in written form for the children to read again.

✔ Encourage the children from the beginning, when listening to build up a picture in their mind of the story or message of the book. Listening to tape or oral reading from time to time can help to stimulate this 'visualizing of the story'.

✔ Use a large-format book or large picture book, and gather the group of children as close around you as possible. One of the great breakthroughs of literacy is the moment when a child realizes that the words you are reading aloud are not in the illustration, but in the black squiggles on the page. They can learn this by watching you closely as you read aloud. You can help this by pointing to the beginning of each line as you read.

✔ Get the children to share in the reading with you. Read a sentence, then ask them to reread it as you point to the beginning of the line and later to each word. Read together in unison. Let the children read repeated patterns, while you fill in the words they do not know. Afterwards, let them work in pairs or small groups to reread the text, with one using a pointer to point to the words. In this way, you can provide the model and let them practise in a risk-free situation.

Predictable Reading

Picture books

Prediction plays an important role in all reading, at any age. As we read, we use our prior knowledge of the subject and the language in order to predict what is coming next. Picture books can help children to form expectations of a text and allow them to predict not only meanings, but individual words.

Talk with the children about the pictures before reading. Ask them to identify the characters and work out what is happening. Then, read the text. Afterwards, make the picture book available for the children to read the story by themselves.

Comic strips are a special kind of picture story. Children can look at the frames of a comic strip and tell their own story. They can use the pictures to help them to interpret the print.

Predictable stories and poems

Many stories have predictable language, such as 'Once upon a time ...' and 'They all lived happily ever after.' Fairy tales have predictable characters, such as princes and princesses, wicked witches and woodcutters' sons. They have predictable settings, like forests, cottages and castles. They use predictable scenarios, such as magic spells, talking animals and happy endings. The more predictable a story, the easier it is to read.

Poems and rhymes also have highly predictable elements, as the rhythm and rhyme scheme gives clues to what the words are likely to be. Rhymes will also draw children's attention to spelling patterns.

You can also make stories more predictable by grouping them together in themes: either by topic, characters, or genre.

Repeated sentence patterns

Reading a repeated sentence pattern gives children the confidence that they can succeed. It will also enable them to begin matching what they say with words on the page and help them to recognize individual words.

Many poems have repeated sentence patterns. Note the repetitions in, 'The House That Jack Built'. Alphabet books typically repeat patterns like, 'A is for ...'. Look out for traditional songs that use repetition, such as, 'The wheels on the bus go round and round', or 'London Bridge is falling down ...'.

Many books for beginning readers are based on a repeated sentence pattern. Collect as many of these as you can. You can also write your own, with the help of the children, using patterns like these:

✔ I like ...
✔ This is my ...
✔ A ... is big.
✔ I wish I could ...

As the repeated words are usually high-frequency words, it is a good way for the children to learn them as sight words.

Memory reading

We can use the oral tradition that students bring with them to school to let them know what real reading is like. Use nursery rhymes, skipping rhymes, jingles, slogans or songs that the children know by heart. If they do not know traditional rhymes, teach the rhymes first. Once the children own the language, they can start to read it.

Print a rhyme the children know on the board or chart paper. As the children chant the rhyme, point to the beginning of each line. In successive readings, point to each individual word. Make the rhyme available for the students to read in small groups or individually. As they finger-point, they will start to match what they say with what they see, and come to recognize individual words and phrases.

Some parents may denigrate the "memory reading" as "not real reading." Tell parents that it is important for children to look for meaning right from the start, and to see themselves as successful readers. Reassure parents that with more practice their children will start to recognize words and come closer to reading the actual text in front of them.

Language experience

This technique uses the children's own experiences written down as their reading material. You, another child, a reading buddy or an adult volunteer can write a "story" that a child dictates. A story a child has experienced, written in the child's own language, is highly predictable.

Guided reading

One of the main benefits of guided reading is that it allows children to revisit and reinforce ground covered in shared sessions. Through directed activities the children are given impetus to read and reread the text several times.

Define the task

With the children, set goals and expectations before they read. Ask them to read a passage of text with a specific purpose in mind.

Example

✔ Find specific information	"Who was the first person Alice met in Wonderland?"
✔ Answer a question	"How did Alice get into Wonderland?"
✔ Look for cause or effect	"What made Alice shrink down so small?"
✔ Find proof	"Was Alice justified in saying the Mad Hatter was rude?"
✔ Make a judgment	"How would you describe Alice's character?"

Chunk the text	Divide the text into smaller, meaningful units and read them one at a time. This is like dividing a novel into chapters. Work with the children before and after the reading of each 'chunk' to find and reflect on specific pieces of information.

✔ "Read the first page, and then we'll talk about the kind of person Ranjit is."
✔ "Read the next paragraph and find out what caused the fire."

Share in the reading

Read aloud the first paragraph or page and then ask the children to read the next for themselves. In this way, children may become familiar with the author's language and style, meet the characters and gain enough prior knowledge of the content to use context cues more effectively as they continue reading. They will also begin to use your voice patterns as a model for intonation and expression.

When children are setting out to read a small chunk or paragraph that you have designated, read the first sentence aloud for them. This is often a topic sentence and can help the children to form expectations and make predictions about the meaning.

Teach children reading skills specifically needed for a text

Different texts require different kinds of reading. A recipe demands we read every word in sequential order; to read a dictionary this way would be self-defeating. Guide children's reading with specific instructions, such as:

✔ "Look at the Table of Contents, and see which chapter deals with dog training."
✔ "Read the side headings and find the section about toads. Then read that section and find three things toads eat."
✔ "Skim the pages and find the conversation between Jack and the giant. Read the conversation to discover the words used in the giant's rhyme."
✔ "Read the first line of each paragraph, and find the one that describes the jungle. Read that paragraph to find out what we should put in our mural."

Introduce vocabulary before reading

This is not so that new words can be memorized before reading. However, if you use some of the vocabulary in pre-reading talk and print one or two interesting words on the board, children are more likely to expect the words and be able to work them out from the context in their reading.

✔ "This poem is called 'Johnny the Juvenile Juggler'. What do you think 'juvenile' means?"

In reading non-fiction, referring to the glossary or index first can forewarn children of difficult or technical words before they meet them independently.

Guided reading of non-fictional material

Because non-fiction material is not often read sequentially like fiction, a good habit to encourage in children is the idea of a 'broken read'. The break may come simply from breaking off for discussion or reflection. It may come from asking children to begin reading at different points in a text before sharing and summarizing what they have read. A 'broken read' can also be 'forced' by employing one of the Directed Activities Related to Text (DARTs) suggested through the 'Effective Use of Reading' project.

Directed Activities Related to Text

✔ Underlining or highlighting.

✔ Labelling.

✔ Cloze procedure (missing out key words).

✔ Questioning.

✔ Sequencing or segmenting a text.

✔ Modelling or representing information in diagram or tabular form.

✔ Summarizing.

These tasks may be used during or after the initial reading of the text. Alternatively, use some of them before the children read. This can act as an 'advance organizer', helping the children to tune into the text before they begin reading. Discuss with the children what they have learned from these activities and how they helped (or hindered) their understanding. This can also underline the relevance of taking parts or the whole of a text and manipulating it to our own ends.

Reading out loud

Reading buddies

A reading buddy can be another child who is a fluent reader, a parent volunteer or an older child. The buddy is there to read aloud, to read along with, to listen, to help in any way needed. Reading buddies need to build up a relationship of trust, so that the child can read in a risk-free situation; keep buddy teams together for extended periods of time. Set up a regular time and place for the buddies to work together. The best way to train reading buddies is to model the kinds of things you want them to do; they can then role play being you.

Reading buddies can help by doing some of these:

✔ Listen to their buddy read without jumping in to correct every time a miscue is made.
✔ Read aloud.
✔ Read in unison.
✔ Share in reading in role.
✔ Help with difficult words.
✔ Help new English speakers learn new vocabulary.
✔ Help children to record what they have read.

✔ Help with follow-up activities.
✔ Help to proofread and edit writing.
✔ Talk about books, authors and personal preferences.
✔ Help with book selection and library visits.
✔ Model a love of reading.

Buzz-group reading

A group or the whole class can read aloud at the same time. They should not attempt to start together or keep together, nor should they listen to one another. They should keep their voices quite low, but can read with expression, use voices for the dialogue, add sound-effects and so on. As the children read, you can unobtrusively glance and listen around the group, noting who is reading fluently, who is hesitant, who is in difficulty. Practising this kind of reading regularly can help children to screen out extraneous noise when they are reading so that they become absorbed in their own reading and imagination.

Reading in role

If a story is mostly dialogue, children can assign parts for the characters, plus one for a narrator and read the selection as a script. The group size will be the number of characters plus the narrator. After reading through, group members can change parts and read again. As they take turns to play different roles, they will be rereading many times, improving their fluency each time. This can also promote good listening habits, as children need to pay close attention to the text while others are reading, so that they can pick up their own cues.

Sometimes one group might rehearse a dramatic reading to share with another group or the whole class. Alternatively, several groups might each prepare a reading of one section, then perform them in sequence to read the selection as a whole.

Reading in role makes it necessary to understand the characters, their moods and their attitudes towards the situations in which they find themselves. The repetitions involved will give children opportunities for these understandings to grow and develop.

Choral reading

This is one way of giving children the opportunity to read a text many times without getting bored with it. It has a long oral tradition in work chants and songs, nursery rhymes, games and skipping rhymes, for example. Repetitions help children who are not fluent readers to access a text and gain confidence in a low-risk situation; every child can enjoy the fulfilment of sharing in a fluent and expressive reading experience.

Choral reading helps comprehension, because the dramatic reading goes beyond facts and information to highlight meaning, emotions and mood. As many of us learned in the early years, we need to know the 'tune' of reading as well as the words. Children will also learn the function of punctuation as a cue to reading. As well as improving their reading, children also learn to: pay attention and pick up cues; follow instructions; work together in groups; and take pride in a polished group presentation.

You can help the children to appreciate the 'tune' of reading through music and rhythm. Younger children could start with nursery rhymes, playground chants and songs they already know. Older children can use pop songs, cheerleader chants, television jingles, or rap.

Alternative forms of choral reading

✔ In unison – everyone reads together. Clear speech is important here, and children can learn to articulate well, follow directions and work as a coherent group. Children use this technique in their skipping rhymes and you can use ones the children already know as an introduction to this technique.

✔ Parts – allocate words or lines to individuals, pairs and small groups. Assign lines for logical reasons, such as different voices for characters or sound effects. This is a little like making a text into a script. It can be adapted to a 'round' chant as children gain experience.

✔ Call and response – divide the group into two parts which 'talk' and 'respond' to one another, perhaps as question and answer, or as opposing voices. This is the technique we use to tell 'knock, knock' jokes.

✔ Cumulative – one person starts, with other voices added gradually until everyone is involved. As the volume increases, so does the feeling of excitement and intensity. If you add voices, then drop them off until only one is left, you can create a feeling of advancing and retreating, of rising and falling, of tension and release. This effect is often created with music in film soundtracks, and can highlight the climax of the action.

✔ Ostinato – add a 'harmony' as a background to the reading. In a marching poem, for example, while one group reads, another group might chant, 'left, right, left right', softly, getting louder, fading away in the distance. This helps children to become aware of rhythm and timing, as they keep pace with the readers.

Techniques to teach choral reading

✔ Have a leader or conductor, yourself or a child, to keep the group together and give cues.

✔ Put your text on an overhead projector, chalkboard or chart paper and use symbols to mark volume, pauses and so on. Use colors to mark different group parts. You can link this with lessons on musical notations, as well as with punctuation marks.

✔ Each time children repeat the piece, add variety in volume, speed, tone and voices. Add one new effect at a time.

✔ Read from different points of view. The same dialogue might be read in anger, in sorrow, sarcastically; as a child, mother, or monster, for example.

✔ When you divide the group into smaller units, use different volume and tone in each group, such as: high voices against low voices; loud against soft; angry against pacifying.

✔ Add sound effects, such as wind blowing, doors slamming, footsteps advancing and retreating.

✔ Use rhythm instruments or clapping to accent a beat or control speed.

✔ Add movement, such as marching, gestures, waving in the wind.

✔ Use minimal costumes and props, such as hats, masks and sticks.

✔ Use recorded or live music as a background to set mood and control speed and rhythm.

Readers' Theatre
You can group several choral selections together, along with a few solo readings, and perform them for yourselves or for an outside audience. This is called Readers' Theatre. Readers' Theatre provides an opportunity to revisit choral pieces that the children have practised in the past, and polish them even further. It makes an excellent presentation for an assembly, concert or parents' evening.

— Techniques to present Readers' Theatre —

✔ It is not usual or necessary for children to memorize pieces; this is a reading activity. However, you will find that children will remember many of their favorite poems.

✔ Invite an outside audience, or perform just for the group members.

✔ Performers can stand in a semicircle, and step into the middle when it is their turn to read.

✔ Performers can stand in a line with their backs to the audience, then turn to face the audience when they read.

✔ Performers can form a tableau suitable to their presentation as they read.

✔ You can provide minimal costumes and props, such as a hat, a walking stick, a cape.

✔ The other children can provide sound effects or movement for another group's performance, such as swaying in the wind, hiding their faces, forming tableaux, or beating time.

✔ The performance can look very professional if children memorize the order of readings and present them without introduction, instructions or a conductor.

Rehearsed oral reading

Fluent, expressive oral reading is a satisfying and useful skill to have, both for children and adults. However, a child stumbling through an oral reading of a piece of text is frustrating and embarrassing for the reader and the listener.

The best way to become skilled in oral reading is through rehearsal. Professional readers, such as television newscasters and actors, do not read in public without rehearsal. They view oral reading as a performance that needs the same preparation and thought in interpretation as a script. This is a good view to take with children. An added benefit of rehearsing an oral reading is that preparing an oral performance requires thought about the meaning, characters, style and mood of the piece.

Opportunities for rehearsed oral reading

✔ Hold a story circle, perhaps once a week. At a story circle, children who wish may rehearse a piece to read aloud, either from a book or a piece of their own writing. Provide a sign-up sheet several days ahead of time. Insist on out-loud rehearsal, which may be to their reading partner or group. Set a time limit of perhaps five minutes and keep to it strictly. When it is time for the performance, the children can sit in a circle or the reader can come to the front. One child can be the host, and introduce each performer and the title of the piece. Keep a record of children who participate and provide other opportunities for those who do not.

✔ Have a current events time. Children can take turns in small groups to select and read interesting clips from the local or national newspapers.

✔ Children can practise and read aloud messages, letters and so on that come to the classroom.

✔ Children can do book talks, at which they read aloud a short excerpt from a book and then discuss it.

✔ The children can rehearse and perform a puppet play from a script. They can adapt a story that is written mostly in dialogue, or write a script of their own.

✔ Children can tape-record stories for others to listen to. Listening privately to their own voices on tape will give them useful feedback on their oral reading performance.

✔ Some children will not be fluent enough to give a good oral performance that others can listen to, or may be too shy to try. These children can read aloud in more informal situations, to small groups or other individuals, or even to puppets or dolls.

Independent reading

Read along with a tape

Children may listen to the whole selection first, before reading along with the tape as many times as they need to. Passages that are too difficult the first time through will become more fluent with repetition. The children can read along independently, or in small groups; it is a risk-free situation, as they will be concentrating on the tape and on their own reading, rather than another's. Afterwards, the children may be able to read the selection independently.

Read to a puppet

This gives a child an opportunity to read aloud in a non-threatening way without a critical audience. Children might enjoy taking turns, with the puppet 'reading' certain passages, alternate paragraphs, or using a special voice for one of the characters.

Read silently

Children who are able can do this sight unseen; others might read independently after experiencing the text in one or more of the other ways first. USSR (Uninterrupted Sustained Silent Reading), DEAR (Drop Everything And Read) or ERIC (Everyone Reads Including the Caretaker) sessions may be set into the working day. These are short sessions in which everyone in the school, adults and children, cease all other work for an uninterrupted independent reading session. Schools often devise their own acronyms to describe such sessions, for example STAR – Stop Talking And Read. In an increasingly crowded Primary working day, these sessions have become much more difficult to arrange, but their importance lies in enabling children to see the adults, including any visitors, reading for pleasure and enjoyment alongside them. It has the additional value that it gives the adult staff an opportunity to keep up to date with current children's reading choices. Generally, the choice of material is left to personal preference. Newspapers, reference or information books are all valid choices in addition to fiction, so long as they involve sustained attention. For children who are less confident or motivated, shorten the amount they read alone.

Chapter 5

Developing comprehension

Comprehension of a text evolves before, during and after the reading experience. After reading is the time when we can help children to think about a text and delve into its many levels of meaning. We can also help them to apply the knowledge they have gained, relate it to their own experience and extend their learning into talking and writing.

Comprehension is usually defined in terms of the following categories:

✔ **Literal**
  Finding facts and details specifically mentioned in the text: "How did Dorothy's house get from Kansas to Munchkinland?"

✔ **Inferential**
  Reading between the lines; using text information to infer information or opinions: "Do you think Dorothy possessed courage and intelligence? How did she demonstrate these qualities?"

✔ **Evaluative**
  Making and justifying judgments: "Were the Munchkins justified in celebrating the witch's death?"

✔ **Creative**
  Applying meanings to personal life: "What wish would you have asked the Wizard of Oz to grant for you?"

Not all of these categories are applicable to all texts. An instruction manual, for example, is likely to demand literal comprehension in the form of attention to detail and sequence, while an advertisement may require a more evaluative approach.

It is important for children also to know the kinds of thinking and response that are appropriate for each kind of text they read. When should they accept everything they read as truth, and when should they question the motives of the writer? When are they at liberty to form their own viewpoints about their reading? When should everyone agree on what is in the text, and when are reactions likely to vary? Is there always only one correct meaning?

By developing a repertoire of activities involving reflection and response, you can help the children not only to access the deeper meanings in a text, but also to recognize whether what they read is fact or fiction, report or editorial, literal or metaphor.

Ways to develop comprehension

1. Reflecting

Taking a moment to think about what has been read is an important part of comprehension. Inexperienced readers often think that when they have read the print and said the words, their job is over. Reflection is part of the thinking process that brings meaning to a text.

Reflection can form part of many classroom activities and can become a habit with children. They can reflect after a gym activity, a film, an argument, a science experiment or a group task. You can guide reflection by asking some specific questions, such as the following:

✔ "What did you find hard? What did you find easy?"
✔ "If you had to do this task again, what would you do differently?"
✔ "Could this really happen?"
✔ "If you were in this situation, what would you have done?"
✔ "Were the characters right to behave this way?"

Sometimes it will be appropriate for children to share their thoughts with you or one another. They may write in their response journal, while at other times they may just ponder.

Providing a 'story-with-a-twist' can also become a reflective activity. Having read the story of The Three Billy Goats Gruff, children were asked to retell the story from the viewpoint of the Troll. One child decided that the Troll was really an Attendant for The Bridge Corporation and it was 'more than his job's worth' to let these noisy potential vandals go 'Trip, trap, trip, trap. Bang! Bang! Bang!' over his precious bridge!

Focusing on the role played by one character in a story can help the children to begin to identify more personally with them. If children are able to reflect on the actions and motivations of characters within a fictional story, they are more likely to ask similar questions of the characters and personalities they will meet in an historical context.

2. Talking

Teacher-directed questioning

By asking specific questions, you can help children to focus on particular issues and ideas. You can in this way guide their reflection and help them to go beyond the surface features of a selection. It is a good idea to decide which major themes of a story you want to focus on and which supporting details you want to bring out. Do not make the mistake of assuming that children have no prior knowledge. Particularly when reading non-fiction texts, tap their collective knowledge of the topic before they read it. This also helps to focus the minds of those who know little about the topic. Try to include some questions to which you do not already know the answer.

Questioning can revolve around the four different kinds of comprehension. Decide which categories are appropriate to the text, and try to ask questions that demand a range of thinking.

Children's questions

Encourage children to write down, either as they read or during their reflection time, any questions about the selection they would like answered. They can then discuss them in small groups or with the whole class. These might be things they did not understand, aspects they would like to hear other opinions about, hypotheses or predictions. These questions might be listed on a chart, initially by the teacher and then by the children themselves, and referred back to after reading.

Reciprocal questions

Encourage the children to think of questions as they read: "As we read this page/chapter/section, I will think of a question to ask you and you must think of a question to ask me." This could begin as a guided group activity and then be transferred to reading partners.

Group discussion

Once children have had experience of sharing ideas in teacher-directed sessions they can conduct the same kind of discussion in small groups. You may want to start them off by giving each group specific questions to discuss, either all the same topic, or different aspects. You can write the discussion topics on the board, or give each group a written copy. Group size should remain small, so that everyone can have a chance to speak. Four is a good number; more than that and you may find the group splitting into factions, with more than one person speaking at the same time. Children who are shy in large groups will often participate more readily in smaller ones.

Teach children how to conduct a group discussion by setting some guidelines. For example:

✔ Each group should have a leader. The leader decides who is to speak, keeps order and makes sure everyone has a turn.
✔ Everyone must listen when a group member is talking.
✔ A group should have a recorder, to write down what the group decides and what their group will share with the rest of the class.

Dialogue

Children work in pairs, with one telling the story to the other. After the retelling, the listener must fill in any parts that the teller omitted. This promotes careful listening as well as careful recalling.

Telephone

Children work in pairs to hold a telephone conversation. It might begin with "Have you heard about ...?" Children relate the story to one another as if in a conversation. They can prompt one another on the details of the story, ask questions and also learn to share and take turns.

News report

Children prepare a report for the radio news. You can give them a time limit of perhaps one minute, so that they have to plan and rehearse.

Debating

This is a more formal kind of discussion. It may be sparked by articles in magazines, the local press or issues related to school. The debate centres on one issue expressed in the form of a statement. For example:

"This class believes Alice was a troublemaker in Wonderland who caused more problems than she solved."

Two teams of four then each prepare to argue for or against.

Evidence

Finding evidence to support their view will require the children to reread parts of the text, skim for specific information, make and justify judgments, evaluate characters, form opinions and organize information. The debate will also teach children that different interpretations of a text are possible and that personal point of view plays a part in reading comprehension.

Classic debates

Both teams prepare their arguments without knowing which side they will be assigned. This helps to prepare them for the arguments that might be made by the other team. A debate is excellent practice in listening carefully; debaters not only have to make their own statements, but respond to points made by the other team.

Preparation

Children might list points they will bring up and arguments they will use to refute the other team. The teams then alternate, with one speaker from each side making a presentation of not more than two minutes, until each member has had a chance to speak. The debate is then opened to anyone on either team or from the floor. After a set time limit, the whole group votes for or against the statement.

You will need a moderator to indicate whose turn it is to speak and to ring a gong when their time is up. With enough practice, children should be able to carry on a debate by themselves in smaller groups of perhaps one moderator, three speakers per team and four others.

Story circle

A group of about four children sit in a circle or around a table. One child begins the story and speaks one sentence. Then the next child continues the story with the following sentence and so on, continuing around the circle until the story is told. You can vary this by asking children in a group of four to retell the story in only one sentence each. To do this, they must learn to select and convey big ideas, rather than small details. It may take a few false starts and trial runs before the group settles on its four sentences. This kind of planning can lead to storyboard activities (see page 39).

---

3. Writing

Writing is not just a way to show what we have learned, it is also a way of learning. Expressing thoughts and ideas in writing makes us think about them in different ways. We often do far more expansion and clarification in writing than we do in either speech or thought. We can also go back and reread what we have written in order to reconsider and refine our ideas.

When you ask children to write in response to reading, try to vary the kinds of writing they do. This will have the added benefit of giving you opportunities to teach the skills involved in different modes of writing.

Personal, expressive writing	Transactional writing	Poetic, literary writing
Personal letter	Newspaper article	Story
Diary	List	Poem
Memo	Instructions	Script
Email	Chart	Biography
Memoir	Board game	Comic strip
	Invitation	Description

Story tree

Use a large model of a tree. As children retell the story, write each extract on a large 'leaf' and attach it to a branch. As children gain confidence they can write out their own leaves. The leaves can then be used to sequence the story in order. Later, children can role play 'autumn', refining their information so that only the essential 'leaves' remain on the tree. When children work with non-fictional information, the story tree becomes a 'Fact Tree'.

Back cover blurb
Asking children to write a blurb for the back cover of a book is an excellent way of tapping both their understanding of and personal response to a text, whether fiction or non-fiction. Writing a concise review is much more difficult than writing a long one, and requires the children to review all the content and to select the highlights. By asking the children to recommend, or not, the book to their friends, they are also required to summarize the main features. The blurb may also provide an alternative to the traditional book review.

When you ask children to write in response to reading, try to vary the kinds of writing they do. By writing in role as a participant in a story, or by writing their own opinions and ideas, children can reflect on their reading in many different ways. They should use the original text as a reference source for vocabulary or factual information, but will be unable to copy directly since they will need to alter the style and language features to match their new text. Demonstrating how to do this through a shared or guided session can prepare them to try it independently. Many good literary texts will lend themselves to different types of writing. By surveying the possibilities at the planning stage, you can provide opportunities for children to practise their reading and writing skills on what are often shorter blocks of text.

Response journal
Literature is most meaningful if children can relate it to their own experience, or project themselves into the experience of others. Learning is most effective when children can see purpose, relevance and application in what they are studying. Writing reflections down in a journal is one way of clarifying thoughts, setting goals and expectations and working out what you have learned. By guiding children's journal entries at first, you can teach them the kinds of thinking that effective readers do.

You can interest children in writing in journals by asking thought-provoking questions and raising controversial issues; most people have an opinion on many topics and like to express these opinions. Questions should not appear to be a test of what children have understood, nor a check on whether they have really read the story. A useful guideline is never to ask a question to which you already know the answer. Instead, ask for ideas and opinions that will be personal for each child.

You can keep children interested in writing in their journals by reading and responding to them frequently. Respond directly onto the children's pages; they are interested in your opinions too, and you can prompt them to extend and clarify their thoughts. The most productive journals are usually dialogues, rather than monologues. It is a good idea for children to keep their journals handy at all times. However, be careful the journal does not become a writing notebook, used for lengthy follow-up activities. Little and often is a good rule of thumb. Limit journal responses to perhaps five minutes or less.

You can often assess the range and quality of children's writing, as well as their understanding, by reading their journal entries. Remember, though, that the journal entries will be rapid, first-draft writing; you should therefore assess the quality of the content, not the spelling and handwriting. Keep your evaluative comments to yourself; you want journal writing to be completely risk-free, so that children will express themselves without inhibition. There will be many other opportunities to respond to and teach the mechanical aspects of writing.

Starters for journal writing

Children can use their journals before, during and after reading (or any other task they do). They can, for example:

✔ Make predictions and form hypotheses about what might happen.
✔ Formulate questions they would like answered.
✔ Write opinions about characters and their actions.
✔ Share personal experiences related to the literature.
✔ Express feelings and emotions aroused by the story.
✔ Express views and opinions in private.
✔ Project themselves into stories.
✔ Make judgments.
✔ Make comparisons.
✔ List evocative words and phrases.
✔ Jot down points to take to a group discussion.
✔ Summarize what they have discovered or learned.
✔ Note personal tastes.
✔ Make self-evaluative comments.

Storyboard

A storyboard is a shooting plan for the making of a film. It may tell a fictional story, a biography, or be a factual documentary. It may be for real people or cartoon characters. The storyboard includes sketches of what will appear on-screen, with the dialogue or commentary that will accompany it.

As they plan a fictional storyboard, the children will need to:

✔ visualize the setting
✔ summarize and sequence events in the plot
✔ understand the role of the characters.

For a documentary storyboard, they will need to categorize and prioritize information. Storyboarding makes a good group activity, particularly as one way to recall and record factual information or research projects. Groups can divide the content amongst members, working individually on different sections and afterwards combining their efforts to complete the whole.

To get them started, you can give the children some guidelines for building a storyboard (see Storyboard Template, page 72). You may wish to predetermine how many boxes you want them to use. This will prevent the story going on too long, and will also oblige the children to select the main ideas they want to represent.

Storyboard guidelines

✔ List the events or information you want to include.

✔ Put your list in sequential order.

✔ Decide how many sketches you will use.

✔ Put a title on each box that will say what the content will be.

✔ Draw a sketch in each box.

✔ Beside each box, add the commentary or dialogue that will go with it.

The storyboard can be a complete project in itself, or can be used to create an audio-visual presentation:

✔ A film.
✔ A series of slides with a taped soundtrack – this is good for a documentary, particularly with a subject of local interest.
✔ A series of overhead transparencies with a soundtrack – the children can make a picture on each transparency using washable markers. They can rehearse an oral presentation, or tape their commentary.

The storyboard can also become a picture book, with each frame developed into a full-page illustration, with text on the opposing page.

Patterning from literature

Literature provides children with some of the best examples of written language. Children can often use this language as a model for their own writing. As they use the vocabulary and sentence structure that they meet in their reading, children can gain a better understanding and appreciation of the special conventions of written language. This will not only help them in their own writing, but will make reading literature more predictable and therefore more fluent. By using literary devices, such as alliteration, in their own writing, children are likely to have a better appreciation of the literature they read.

Using a simple caption book as a frame for children's own writing helps to provide them with scaffolding around which they can build their own ideas.

Many critics suggest that there is no such thing as an original story, only different variations and sequences for a finite number of plots. This may be demonstrated by looking at the structure of the Fable of the Lion and the Mouse.

The Fable of the Lion and the Mouse

Sequence of main events

✔ The lion is trapped in a net and is struggling to get out.

✔ The bear and the elephant are too frightened to help him.

✔ A mouse arrives and offers help.

✔ By gnawing on the net, the mouse manages to free the lion.

✔ The lion is pleased to be free.

Parallel plot

✔ Someone is in difficulty.

✔ They try to solve the problem by themselves.

✔ They seek help, but others are either unable or unwilling to help.

✔ Help arrives from an unlikely source.

✔ An unusual solution is found.

✔ The problem is solved – happiness and gratitude.

You and the children need to know the story, retell it, discuss the main events and list them in order. This could be done as a class or group activity. Afterwards, the children should discuss how the story's events could be used with a plot for another story, using new characters and settings. This could be done as a class, group or independent activity. You may notice that the plot could easily be transformed into the parable of the Good Samaritan.

Parallel plots are useful for less able readers because the similarity of plots aids prediction. You will find many examples in reading series and in children's fiction.

Translating the text into a new format

One of the best ways to help children to see the application of the skill and strategies they have learned is to present a text in a new form. For example, having read an explanatory account about the training of Guide Dogs for the Blind, the children might design a leaflet for would-be puppy owners.

Information leaflets, advertising flyers and guides

Children may use examples of these in their shared or guided group work to produce their own versions. A book about the work of vets might lend itself to the children producing an information leaflet, designed for their own age group, on pet care. Using a real leaflet as a guide to provide structure allows the children to build or improve on the model.

Some children used a simple three-fold tourist guide on their town to produce their own guide to their school. They substituted sub-headings and illustrations, using the language of the printed guide as the model for their own writing.

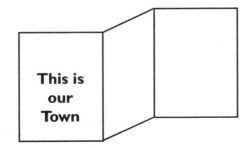

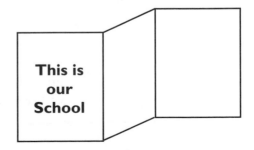

4. Related reading

One reason for grouping readings and activities into a theme is to help children to make connections and gain cumulative knowledge about topics, vocabulary, styles and genres. When children have read a story, poem, article, comic strip or any other kind of writing, they will have gained knowledge of the genre. This will make it easier for them to read another piece that is similar in some aspect. The more experience children have with a genre, and the more they discover about a subject, the greater will be their confidence and fluency in reading similar material.

With the children, you can set up a display or a mini-library of related reading that will remain available for personal reading during the course of the theme.

Ways to promote further reading

✔ Conduct book talks. Show some selections, and give brief information about what each contains. Children can also do book talks.

✔ Read aloud either the opening chapter or an interesting part of the book and invite the children to continue.

✔ Read aloud the book jacket synopsis and add a few details.

✔ Set up a display of reviews and recommendations, some taken from the book jacket, others written by children who have read the book.

✔ Build a child-written card file of reviews for others to use as a reference (see Book Review, page 73). This will provide a real purpose for the writing of book reviews. The file card will keep reviews brief, so that they are not a burden to the writer or reader. You can set up a model for the review, to give children guidelines.

✔ Make contributions to the file voluntary. You may find that children are keener to express their opinions when they can do it in a brief manner.

✔ An annual school 'book week' allows the local community to become involved with the enjoyment of literature. Many schools adopt a special theme and invite readers from the community to join in. Many major companies and sporting institutions now foster literacy projects which may benefit schools and enhance the status of reading.

Choosing related reading

Choose selections that have at least one aspect in common with text that the children are familiar with:

✔ Works by the same author and illustrator.
✔ Other examples of the same genre.
✔ Readings on the same theme or subject.
✔ Reference books on the same theme or topic.
✔ Child-authored material.

5. Drama

From a very young age, children when they are playing, act out situations, create improvisations, role play people around them and try to imitate the world they see; it is their world of 'make-believe'. It is also their way of understanding and making sense of their world. We can extend this kind of meaning-making into reading by enabling children to respond to a story through drama.

The benefits of using drama

✔ Drama can help children to develop reading comprehension and learn to think about their reading on more than a surface level.

✔ It can also help reluctant readers to become more personally involved in a story, and thus more motivated.

✔ Through drama, children can experience a story from the inside and respond emotionally as well as cognitively. Literature is only meaningful to the extent that it touches our lives and influences our thinking.

✔ By role playing, the children can project themselves into the personalities of the characters and the situations they encounter, or into imagined characters and situations. In this way, they can come to understand the motivations of the characters, as well as issues of justice, ethics and fairness.

✔ Through story dramatization and improvisation they can explore events and characters through time, looking at them before, during or after the episode in a selection.

✔ They can bring their own experience to bear on a situation and also extend their experience through the lives of the story characters.

✔ They can experience emotions, examine values, solve problems and make judgments from a different perspective.

✔ Drama can help children to build their own confidence and be more tolerant of other opinions and customs.

✔ Through drama, children can develop their communication skills, use language in many different ways, and learn to work cooperatively.

Responding to literature

The following ideas are outlined briefly, with some examples. You will need to refer to a handbook on drama for a more detailed explanation.

✔ **Dramatic play**
Dramatic play is often associated with younger children, but older children still enjoy "let's pretend." Through dramatic play, children can project into a story, explore issues, understand characters, role-play situations, discuss ideas, solve problems and respond to literature in many other ways. As there is no audience, children can experiment in a risk-free environment.

Provide simple props, such as:
✔ two telephones with notepads
✔ clothing, such as hats, belts, capes, lengths of fabric
✔ walking stick, suitcase, shoebox, magic wand, crown
✔ toys, including buildings, vehicles, people, animals

✔ **Role playing**
Children can be asked to take the role of a character, for example the Troll in the story of The Three Billy Goats Gruff. The class or group may then question the character about his behavior. Perhaps he had a good reason for being so grumpy! "How would you feel if people went 'Trip, trap, trip, trap. Bang! Bang! Bang!' all day on your bridge?"

✔ **Teacher-in-role**
One way to guide the children's role-playing is for you to become part of the drama too. As part of the role-playing, you can ask questions of the characters, focus the children's thinking, change their direction and move the role-playing along. In role, you might:
✔ chair a village meeting at which children are the villagers. Present problems, and invite the children to suggest solutions
✔ be a stranger in town finding out what is going on
✔ be a wizard, changing the appearance or behavior of the townsfolk
✔ be a protagonist in the story, and create a confrontation with other characters.

Training children to work in role

To get children started, give them short tasks with a single focus and clear instructions.

Sample role-play

✔ Work in pairs. One partner assumes the role of a character from a story and, in character, tells one incident from the story. On a predetermined signal, partners switch roles, and the other partner continues the story.

✔ Work in pairs. One partner is a reporter interviewing an eyewitness of an event that takes place in a story. Then other partner asks questions to find out what happened.

✔ Work in groups of four. Each group member assumes the role of an elder in a tribe. Together, they try to solve a problem from a story.

✔ **Storytelling**
Stories children read can become springboards for children either to retell or to develop stories of their own. Children can tell stories with a partner, in a group or to the class. Telling a story or listening to a story being told can give children a better understanding of poetic language and how it can be used.

Children can learn to tell stories by relating incidents that have happened to them. Arrange children into groups of three to four, and give each group a specific topic to tell a story about, perhaps something they saw on a trip, or an incident they witnessed on their way to school.

✔ **Tableaux**

Introduce students to tableau by describing it as a group of still, motionless people arranged to represent a scene. Have children create simple objects first, like geometric shapes, then move onto representing objects like trains, mountains or robots. Establish a signal for children to begin creating a tableau within a specified time, and then a signal for the children to freeze "in position". You can add narration and movement to bring a tableau to life. In a tableau there should be no speech, although speech may be needed during rehearsal.

Children can:

✔ Retell a story by forming a series of tableaux. On a signal, they can move smoothly from one tableau to the next.

✔ Form tableaux as you read a story aloud. Stop reading at significant events in the story to indicate when children should create a tableau. As you continue to read, children can relax and listen.

✔ Narrate or retell a story, while others form tableaux.

✔ Work in groups to form a tableau representing one particular action or event in a story. As the story is read out loud, each group's tableau comes to life at the appropriate time in the story.

✔ Use an instant camera to record a tableau. Children can then use the pictures to extend the activity into writing.

✔ **Movement**

Movement allows children to explore thoughts and feelings through physical action, while developing concentration and control. They can reflect anger, grief, humor or fear through movement and come to understand them on a physical and emotional level. Movement can help children feel the rhythm of language, and serve as a warm-up for other drama activities.

Children can:

✔ Toss an invisible ball back and forth with a partner.

✔ Mirror a partner's actions.

✔ Pretend, on a signal, to be in different environments, such as deep water, high wind, weightlessness, deep sand or a narrow tunnel.

✔ Create movement sequences like a flower opening in the sun and then closing at nightfall; an icicle melting; a balloon inflating slowly, then bursting.

✔ Perform a routine task like climbing a stair, as different creatures: a snake, a frog, a monster or an alien.

✔ Work in groups to pretend to be cogs in a machine, farmers planting seeds in a row, fishermen hauling in nets, trees in a hurricane or robots doing aerobics.

✔ **Mime**
Through mime, children can explore a story without language.

Children can use mime to:
  ✔ Move invisible kittens from one basket to another.
  ✔ Pass an invisible object around a circle. (You can ask the children to change the object from a grape to an orange, and then to a bowling ball.)
  ✔ Wash and dry your hands in an imaginary sink.
  ✔ Get dressed for playing in the snow.
  ✔ Prepare and eat your favorite breakfast.

✔ **Improvisation**
Through improvisation children reflect on a story, identify with the situation and characters and build on these ideas to create a new story. Improvising can be verbal or non-verbal.

To initiate an improvisation, select an incident from a story, pose a problem, place the children in role and let them work in small groups to solve the problem. You can use the following scenario as an example.

Example

You are a four-person rescue team setting out to descend into the rabbit hole to find the missing Alice, from *Alice in Wonderland*. As a group, form a plan for your rescue and then perform your rescue. Decide together what special skill each team member has that will be helpful in your rescue. What equipment will you take with you on your rescue? Once you return, each member of your group will be asked to tell about one of the problems you encountered, and how you solved it.

Sound effects

Adding sound effects to an oral reading helps children to identify details in a story and follow a story line. It necessitates repeated readings and a good understanding not only of the actions taking place, but also of the setting, the timing and the mood. It can add to the children's appreciation of poems and stories as they help bring them to life.

Choose a story or poem with many different kinds of sound. Divide the children into small groups, each one responsible for providing the right sound effect at the appropriate time. For example, they might be the wind building and dying, footsteps approaching, a door creaking, dishes breaking. First the groups decide how they will produce their effect – perhaps with their voices, props or musical instruments. Then you or another child can read the story aloud and let the sounds develop. After a first run through, discuss with the children how the effects worked. Were they believable? Was the volume right? Did they come in on cue? What should be modified? Then you can have another reading. Once you have rehearsed enough, you can tape-record the production, and let the children listen to their own dramatic reading.

Once the children have had some experience adding sound effects, they can work in small groups to produce dramatic readings by themselves.

Puppetry

Through puppets, children can role play in a more impersonal and less threatening way. The anonymity of puppets often encourages shy children to participate and children are often used to improvising dialogue through dolls and toys. Puppets need not be complex; paper cut-outs on sticks or decorated socks are often adequate and can easily be customised to match characters in a particular story.

Using puppets, children can:

✔ read a story
✔ retell a story
✔ work in role
✔ hold a conversation
✔ improvise a dialogue
✔ take opposing sides in an argument
✔ project themselves into a story.

6. Visual representation

Pictures

Creating a picture can be one form of retelling a story, continuing a story, recreating a mood and representing a setting. It can also lead children to reflect on their reading, recall events and details of the plot, understand mood and setting and recognize and understand characters.

A picture can take many forms and be created in many ways. It may be an individual painting or drawing, a group mural, an individual or group collage, or a mobile. It is ideal if you can provide a painting easel that can be available for several children to use at any time. Build up a scrap-box with different kinds of paper for use in cut and paste. You can also have a box of drawing materials, including felt-tip pens, pencils, crayons, pens and chalk.

Sometimes this activity may simply be: "Draw the picture that came into your mind when you read about the wolf falling down the chimney into the cooking pot."

Children can be encouraged to add detail to make their picture more specific. Then they can draw a series of pictures to show the sequence of events in the process. These pictures should be marked on grounds of accuracy or imagination rather than artistic merit.

To make a large group mural, lay a large piece of paper on the floor and have paint stations at convenient locations around it. Each child finds an area of the paper on which to work. First choose a topic or title for the mural. Sometimes, you may just let the children create individual pictures within the mural, somewhat like a collage. At other times, you may want the group to discuss content and form before beginning and assign different aspects to different children. You may ask one group to start the mural and another group to add to it until everyone has contributed. You can combine painting and collage techniques by asking children to paint a background, then to paint or cut out pictures to paste onto it. For some murals, children may add dialogue balloons, labels, place names and so on.

Semantic or concept mapping

Semantic mapping is a way to link ideas and visually represent relationships among events, characters and so on. It is the technique we use to draw our family tree, much like flow-charting. It is particularly helpful for children who are visual learners, as a map shows information graphically.

The concept map below shows information from the index of the book about whales (p. 19) presented under headings.

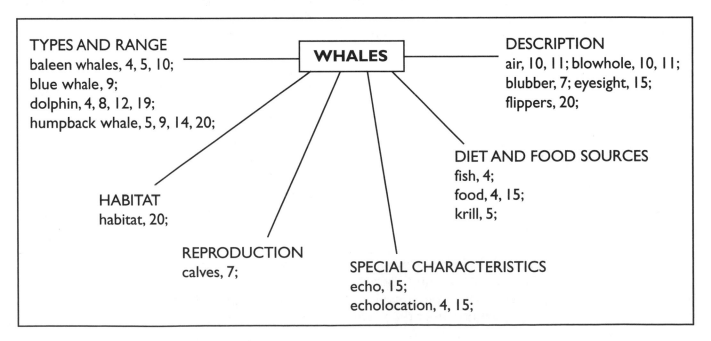

TYPES AND RANGE
baleen whales, 4, 5, 10;
blue whale, 9;
dolphin, 4, 8, 12, 19;
humpback whale, 5, 9, 14, 20;

WHALES

DESCRIPTION
air, 10, 11; blowhole, 10, 11;
blubber, 7; eyesight, 15;
flippers, 20;

HABITAT
habitat, 20;

DIET AND FOOD SOURCES
fish, 4;
food, 4, 15;
krill, 5;

REPRODUCTION
calves, 7;

SPECIAL CHARACTERISTICS
echo, 15;
echolocation, 4, 15;

Mapping techniques

✔ Sequence events in a story by writing significant events along a road, railway track, a ladder, or by adding pieces to a kite tail. Choose a visual image that fits the theme of the story, such as The Yellow Brick Road or the leaves on Jack's beanstalk.

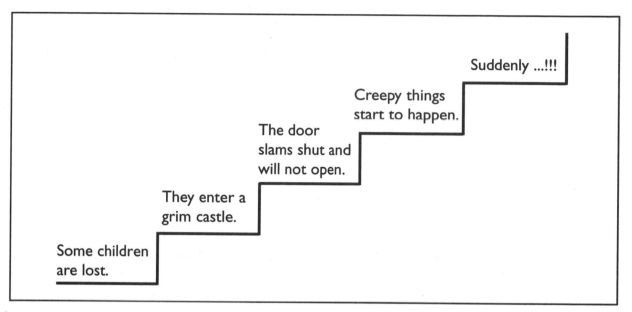

Suddenly ...!!!

Creepy things start to happen.

The door slams shut and will not open.

They enter a grim castle.

Some children are lost.

✔ Draw the spokes of a wheel and put a title or heading at the hub. On each spoke, write one aspect of the topic, for example characters, settings, events and emotions. Each spoke can then be divided to continue with details, in the manner of a flow-chart. This will build a visual map of the main features of a story.

✔ Map the build-up of excitement or mystery on a staircase. Start at the bottom step with the first significant event, and add one on each step until the denouement is reached on the landing.

✔ Build up a series of 'mountain ranges' using the peaks and valleys of the plot. Children can record the ups and downs of tension and release, mystery and ensuing solutions. This will show the rise and fall of the plot.

✔ Make a character map in the form of a tree. Write the name of each character on a major branch. When the children learn something new about a character, they can add smaller branches.

✔ Map cause-and-effect relationships using linked pairs of objects, such as a tugboat and a ship, a horse and cart, a car and trailer. Children can print the cause on the first object and the effect on the second.

Posters

Making posters gives children an opportunity to represent transactional writing: for example, Kate advertises for pirates to join her crew. By making a poster based on a story or a non-fiction selection, such as an instruction manual, less confident children have a real reason to scan the text for relevant information before presenting it in a different form. Making a poster may be less threatening to them than writing continuous prose.

Models

Children can construct three-dimensional representations of a character, mood or event from a story by using recycled materials. Collect items such as cardboard tubes, boxes, string, straws, rubber bands, wallpaper scraps, washers and buttons.

A diorama is a particular kind of model. It looks like a stage setting, and can represent the setting of a book, a room or an event; it is a frozen moment from a story. To build a diorama, the children will need to read for detail, make notes and plan ahead.

Masks

Children can make masks from a variety of materials to portray a physical representation of a character or a mood. Making the mask requires careful reading for details, and also an understanding of the character's role in the story. The children can use their masks to create a display or to illustrate a written character sketch. Masks can also be used for readers' theatre, role-playing, tableaux and choral dramatization.

Reasons for using response activities

Having a repertoire of ways for children to reflect and respond to reading will not only make your classroom a more interesting place, it will also give students a variety of ways to think, talk, read and write. It provides an opportunity for:

✔ children of differing abilities and learning styles to find their own ways of making sense of what they read
✔ children to respond individually, in small groups and in larger groups
✔ many different kinds of writing, and will give you the opportunity to teach the writing skills needed for each task
✔ teachers to link reading, writing, art and other subjects in a common theme
✔ teachers to guide children's thinking about their reading to ensure that they develop a wide range of skills
✔ reluctant readers to gain ideas, support and confidence through working in groups
✔ reluctant writers to reflect and respond, and contribute to the class effort
✔ children whose native language is not English to find their own ways to participate.

Chapter

6

Developing language skills

It is possible to understand the written word without ever being able to decode it. What is not possible, for those with limited decoding skill, is to become **independent**. Developing comprehension skills and strategies for literature and information will only be truly successful if children are able to **take control** of the process themselves. For this they will need skills and strategies in deciphering and interpreting the print on the page. These strategies and skills need to develop alongside the comprehension work so that as children meet new and varied texts, they are able to use these strategies in increasingly flexible ways.

Vocabulary

Listening to a text read aloud

Reading aloud provides a good opportunity to expose children to language beyond their own reading level. Children's listening vocabularies are likely to be more extensive than their reading vocabularies. Hearing the expression and intonation of a skilled oral reader can help children to work out a word from its context. Do not limit the language of talking and reading to words which the children already know.

Key points

- ✔ Read aloud to children as often as possible, even when they are capable of reading for themselves. Freeing the mind from the decoding task allows it to focus on the pictures and messages evoked.
- ✔ Use the opportunity to give a 'performance' of the text, adding as much animation and change of pitch and pace as possible to demonstrate how it should be done.
- ✔ Encourage the children to work together to unlock or decode words in the text, using what they know to make sense of what they don't know.
- ✔ Ensure that children know the correct terms for the parts of a book. Confidence comes from knowing what features to expect.
- ✔ Ask questions in advance of reading to help the children to pay attention to particular aspects.
- ✔ Make a slight pause to hold suspense or to indicate conventions of story structure.
- ✔ Collect useful beginnings, endings or powerful extracts from specific stories and display them with correct references so that the children can find the book again.
- ✔ Read short extracts from books which the children might read on in guided sessions or for themselves.
- ✔ Emphasize particular rhythms and rhyme patterns to help the children to predict their occurrence.
- ✔ Refer back to the author or illustrator as a real person, for example "Why do you think Ruth Brown chose this word?"

Extending vocabulary

Children, in fact all of us, have different vocabularies for reading, writing, speaking and listening. There are many words that we understand when we hear them which we would not use in our own speech. We can work out the meaning of many words in reading that we would not use in our own writing. For many of their activities, children need to feel free to use their own language and vocabulary. This is particularly true for personal, expressive writing and talking. However, we also want to expand the children's knowledge of the meanings, origins and functions of words.

Young children learn new words by hearing them in context. They then try them out, and judge by the feedback they get whether they have communicated correctly, modifying their language as they go along. Children will infer the meaning of many new words from context as they read and also as they listen to the oral language of the classroom. By using words in a natural way as we go about our day-to-day classroom activities, we can make them familiar for the children.

We can also sometimes make words a specific focus for teaching and discussion: explaining their meanings, exploring their etymology, looking at their spellings and experimenting with ways to use them.

Focus on interesting words

Both you and the children can pick out words from the reading selection that you find interesting, or ones that they may not understand. Find out and explain what you can about the words – their prefix, root and suffix, as well as their language of origin. List other words that are related in meaning. Keep an ongoing list of words special to a particular piece of reading, such as place names, foreign words or technical terms.

Keep all your lists handy for the children to use as a reference when they are writing.

Make a word mobile

The children can collect a number of words, print them on cards and hang them with thread from wire coat hangers to make a mobile. They can hang the words individually to make one word family, or list words on different aspects of a topic. For example, words collected on the topic of 'our trip to the zoo' could be listed in categories such as: mammals, birds, reptiles, fish and habitats. This kind of sorting activity is very much like paragraphing, or planning sections of a report. It is also similar to preparing for research and other reading and writing.

Key points

✔ Do not be afraid to use words that children may not yet understand, but do try to give clues to their meaning through the context of what you say. For example, even very young children may be familiar with the word 'assembly', albeit within a very special context.

✔ Value the vocabulary children offer, sometimes extending it in your replies to them. "This glue is sticky!"; "Yes it's sticky and tacky!"

✔ As soon as they are able, encourage the children to use a thesaurus to find synonyms for common words they use.

✔ Make collections of words with similar meanings. For example, how many words could you use instead of laugh, cry, said? Once collections have been made, discuss which might be appropriate in particular contexts. What would be the difference between 'the children chuckled' and 'the children snickered'?

✔ When new terminology, for example 'consonant', is being introduced, try to use it in context many times during the course of a day or week. Encouraging the children to repeat it is desirable, but do not expect them to use it in their normal speech until it has had time to be absorbed.

✔ Introduce words on a regular basis for children to explore. Some teachers like to write a particular word, for example 'bank' or 'elicit', on the board. The children must find out as much as they can about the word and its meanings, by research or by asking friends or family, and then use it correctly in their speech or writing. Unusual words might be alternated with simple words that have varied meanings.

✔ Try a 'star word of the week' board in which the children as well as their teachers are encouraged to display a word to be explored.

✔ Make up a rap or word rhythms using words with a similar pattern or ending: 'nation, station, legislation, observation, creation', or 'breeze, squeeze, freeze'.

✔ Read aloud poetry with imaginative, alliterative or onomatopoeic words and encourage the children to learn part or all of them.

✔ Discuss how the meaning of words may change within generations, for example 'wicked', and encourage the children to explain or define words from their peer culture.

✔ Play games with words, trying spoonerisms (chish and fips) or malapropisms (Are you sure that match is distinguished?) and over-pronouncing tricky spelling patterns (sCissors, FebRuary). Allow the children to correct your 'deliberate' spelling errors.

Spelling through reading

Spelling is a skill of word construction, not word memorization. Good spellers understand how words work and can build them as required. English words come from many different language backgrounds and have evolved over the centuries. Because of this, we can improve our spelling if we know about where words come from, what they mean and how they are constructed. After any reading experience, you can take the opportunity to draw the children's attention to certain words and how they are spelled.

Choose a word with a consonant or vowel combination you wish to teach. Print it on the board, and make sure the children can read the word. Then ask the children to suggest other words that share the same pattern. Older children can work in small groups to collect and list words that belong to the same family. Suggest that the children ask at home for other words belonging to patterns they have studied in class.

Focus on spelling patterns

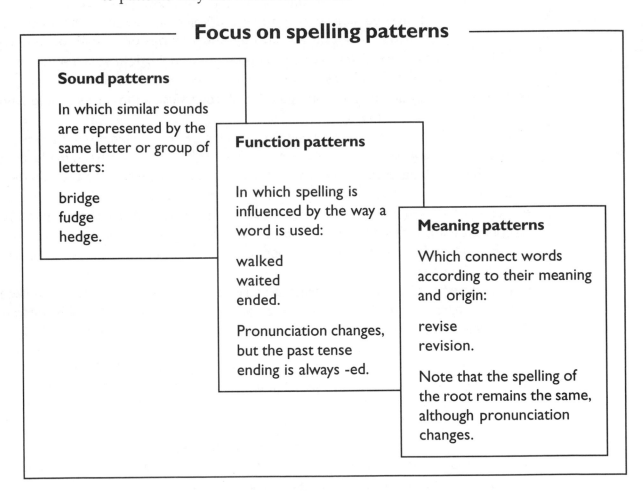

Sound patterns

In which similar sounds are represented by the same letter or group of letters:

bridge
fudge
hedge.

Function patterns

In which spelling is influenced by the way a word is used:

walked
waited
ended.

Pronunciation changes, but the past tense ending is always -ed.

Meaning patterns

Which connect words according to their meaning and origin:

revise
revision.

Note that the spelling of the root remains the same, although pronunciation changes.

Children can keep a growing list of new words that they meet during a theme. Post these in a prominent place during the course of the theme or provide each child with a copy, so that the words are available for the children to use in their own writing. List the words alphabetically, so that the children use their dictionary skills each time they look for a word. Make sure children do not think that this is a list of spellings to memorize; encourage them to use the list as a reference when they are writing or proofreading.

Understanding the 'parts' from which words are made

Many children, even when they can identify each of the single alphabet sounds and the phonemes that make up words, fail to see that these parts can be manipulated when we take control of language. Children may not see that 'sea' is made up of an **onset** (s) and a **rime** (ea). By changing the onset (st) and adding a new ending to the phoneme we create a new **rime pattern** (eam), which makes the word 'steam'. Children can be encouraged to take over control of words by playing word games and making word puzzles. Asking them to make a list of words by changing either the onset or the rime pattern, while keeping the same phoneme, can help them to understand how words are built. In understanding that they can spell 'scream' by knowing the rime pattern for 'dream' and 'cream', children are able to **make an analogy**.

Knowing and using these terms when working with words helps children to understand that the parts of words may be controlled and manipulated.

Simple word webs

Either before or at the end of a whole class shared session, encourage the children to work together to play with word families, making simple word webs. Encourage them to work through in alphabet order trying and rejecting 'words' by changing onsets, adding new endings or suffixes or new prefixes.

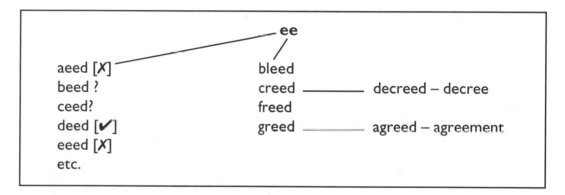

In their guided or independent activities the children could then work with a dictionary to check which of their queries are real words or not. Less able children will often find it helpful physically to make the words using plastic letters or letter cards.

Children also need to know that long words are made up of syllables. Encouraging them to play with syllables can be the precursor of understanding the role of prefixes and suffixes. Ask the children to take 'car-a-van' and make nonsense vehicles, such as: train-a-boat, bus-a-bike, tram-a-trolley, and then illustrate them.

Blending

The vocal machinery of children of Primary school age is still developing, and many children will have difficulty pronouncing some of the blends, especially at the beginning of words, for example 'must' and 'stir'. Particularly with three-letter blends children will often insert a hidden vowel or 'schwa' sound. Thus '**str**ing' can become 'st**ir**ring', especially if the word is encountered in isolation and out of context. This does not mean that the children cannot recognize and match the pattern by sight.

Although the ultimate aim must be for children to recognize common words instantly both in and out of context, there are steps which can assist the less able child. Ask the children to make nonsense words using plastic letters. They should change the vowel each time. Once they have made a set, they should read them aloud to a partner. As they gain confidence they can be asked to read them as quickly as possible. The resulting tongue-twisting causes great hilarity but helps them to develop a perception of what is sense and what is nonsense.

blab	bleb	blib	blob	blub
blad	bl_d	bl_d	blod	blud
blat	bl_t	blit	bl_t	bl_t

Learning about syllables

One of the most vital skills in reading is the ability to split a word into its parts. Often children who have achieved the first stages of phonic skill, that of recognizing the main sounds and blends, will still stick on a plateau in terms of their development because of their lack of skill in syllabification. As soon as children recognize the difference between vowels and consonants, they should begin to split words up. Teachers may find it helpful to begin with simple compound words, such as car/pet, sun/light, star/fish, to demonstrate the knack of identifying the vowels and marking syllable boundaries.

Because the syllable boundaries are much easier to distinguish once you can read and understand the principle of roots, prefixes and suffixes, it is sensible to begin by marking boundaries in words the children can already read or are likely to find memorable. 'Hippopotamus' is an excellent example of a seemingly complicated word which is made up of simple parts. Again, practice in physically building words can assist children when it comes to breaking these words down in reading and can also reveal some of the 'tricky bits' which may cause problems in spelling.

Working with a group of children, each of whom has a set of plastic letters or letter cards, ask them to build words in parts: cat-er-pill-ar, bib-li-o-graph-y, re-mem-ber, hes-i-tate. You may then discuss the rules governing each part of the word, whether vowels are long or short, and why.

Call My Bluff!

As children begin to learn about the roots and derivatives of words, a game based on the idea of the television game, *Call My Bluff*, can act as the precursor to more formal work on prefixes and suffixes. Children will often display an implicit understanding of how words work which is far beyond their independent reading stage.

Take a nonsense root word, for example 'whipple', and ask the children to play a game, imagining a meaning for the word in their minds. They must not reveal this meaning to the rest of the class. Then ask them to think of answers to the following questions:

✔ Is it a noun or a verb? – **A** whipple or **to** whipple?

> *A lesser spotted whipple.*
> *The boy whippled noisily after school.*

✔ What would it mean if you said something was 'whipply'?
✔ Could you have a 'whipply' day?
✔ Why might someone be called a 'whippler'?
✔ And could you be 'dewhippled', 'unwhippled' or 'diswhippled', and what would be the difference?

> *How did it feel to be diswhippled?*

Later, as children begin to extend their knowledge of different prefixes and suffixes, they might speculate on the meaning of: a 'whipplologist'; 'whipplation'; an 'anti-whippling' society or what might happen in a 'whipplectomy'?

> *I want to be a whipplologist when I grow up!*

All of these, of course, demand the application of spelling rules and conventions to be applied to their creation.

> *Down with whippling!*

Use new words in context

If you want children to learn words that they will continue to use, such as technical language or science words, try to use the words in context frequently. It is much easier to talk to children if they know the correct terminology of a subject.

Similarly, it is easier to talk to children about their writing if they know the technical terms of grammar. Young children will have learned the technical language terms 'word' and 'sentence' because they have heard them in context many times a day in their early school life; they will probably never hear a definition of either, but will understand and use them correctly. They can learn other technical terms like 'adjective' and 'simile' just as readily, as long as they hear them used in context many times and have many opportunities to use these terms themselves. For example, you can draw children's attention to a descriptive passage from a story and ask them which adjectives express the mood well. Then ask them to look at the adjectives they have used in their own story.

Look at the parts of words

Children might do this by looking at a word's root, and connecting it with other similar words they know. They might look at the suffix and work out the part of speech. They might know the function and meaning of the prefix. By doing this, children will not only learn new words, they will also learn how words are constructed and how they can use a knowledge of one word to work out the meaning of many new words for themselves.

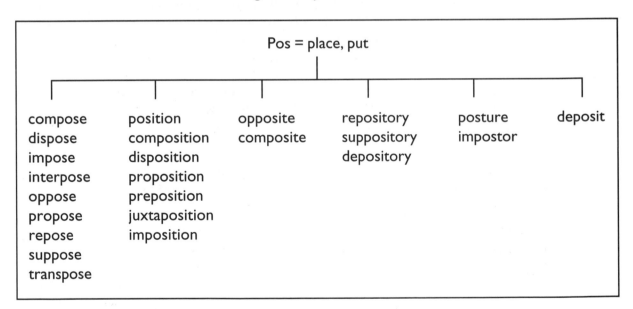

Pos = place, put

compose	position	opposite	repository	posture	deposit
dispose	composition	composite	suppository	impostor	
impose	disposition		depository		
interpose	proposition				
oppose	preposition				
propose	juxtaposition				
repose	imposition				
suppose					
transpose					

Give a definition

Sometimes you will want to draw the children's attention to a word and explain what it means. Whenever you do this, it is a good idea to list other related words, such as words that use the same root or share a spelling pattern. You can then demonstrate how to use the new word by giving examples and asking the children to come up with more.

Tell word stories Tell children about the origins of words, where they come from and how their meanings have developed over time. Good sources for such stories are etymological dictionaries and books about word histories. For example, the words 'hospitable' and 'hostile', seemingly opposites, are actually related and are derived from the same Latin word, *hospes*, meaning both a guest or visitor and one who provides for a guest or visitor. The word 'host' came to mean also a stranger and eventually an enemy.

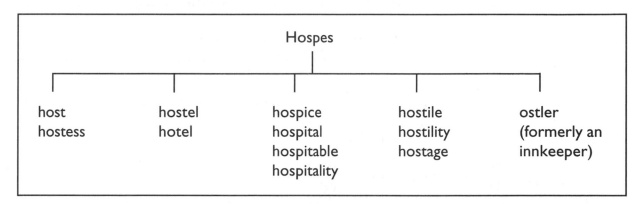

Collect theme words Themes often introduce children to terminology and technical language that they are not familiar with. For example, collecting rocks may introduce words like 'sedimentary' and 'geologist' and they can use these to start their own word families.

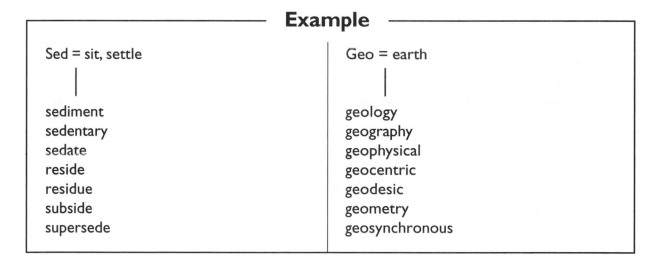

Build word families

With the children, you can build lists of words that have a connection with one another. They might be words that share the same root or prefix, or synonyms or antonyms, or rhyming words that have the same spelling pattern and so on. You can make a list, or build a word web, semantic map or flow-chart. Children can often learn the meaning and spelling of new words by linking words together in 'families'.

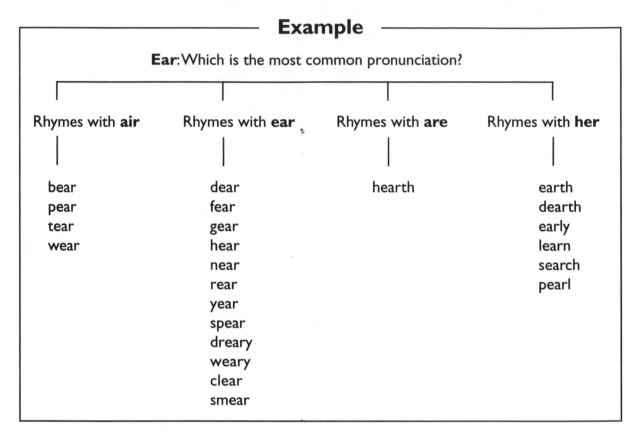

Example

Ear: Which is the most common pronunciation?

Rhymes with **air**	Rhymes with **ear**	Rhymes with **are**	Rhymes with **her**
bear	dear	hearth	earth
pear	fear		dearth
tear	gear		early
wear	hear		learn
	near		search
	rear		pearl
	year		
	spear		
	dreary		
	weary		
	clear		
	smear		

Make a word collage

With the children, brainstorm a list of words suggested by: a theme, a story, a character, the weather and so on. You can simply make a list of words, or categorize them by topic, part of speech, attitude or opinion, for example. The children can print each word on a separate piece of paper and paste them on a background to form a collage. Familiarity with the words may help children to read them and use them in their writing.

Chapter 7

Encouraging reluctant readers

Tackling reluctant reading

Mark Twain once observed that if a cat sat on a hot stove it would never sit on a hot stove again – or a cold one. Once something becomes an unfriendly object, we tend to avoid contact with it. For some children, books are unfriendly objects and reading becomes a subject that can lead to embarrassment and failure.

Even for children who read willingly, the time spent reading in class is very short. We use this time as best we can to model the process, teach the skills and give children as much practice as we can. However, this will never be enough to build fluent readers. We also need to foster a love of reading, so that children will become lifelong readers. When children enjoy reading, they will spend time reading out of school, and will see books as a source of pleasure and information.

There can be many reasons why some children are reluctant readers, but they fall into two main categories:

✔ The children are not successful in making meaning when they read. This leads to a sense of inadequacy and poor self-esteem.
✔ The children do not find reading interesting. When given a choice, they will choose activities other than reading.

Talk to the children to find out how they feel about reading. Ask questions such as these:

✔ "Do you think you are a good reader?"
✔ "What do you do well?"
✔ "What do you find difficult?"
✔ "Do you look forward to reading time?"
✔ "What reading activities do you enjoy?"
✔ "What reading activities do you not like?"
✔ "How do you feel when you are asked to read aloud?"
✔ "Do you read at home? What do you read?"
✔ "Do you like receiving books as gifts?"
✔ "What books or stories have you enjoyed?"

Promoting self-esteem

✔ Provide a risk-free climate.

✔ Do not ask children to read aloud unless they have had enough time to rehearse.

✔ Give children feedback and evaluation in private.

✔ Know what you can expect of each child. Do not demand more than a child can deliver. This builds in failure from the start.

✔ Ask the children to work in mixed-ability groups on a frequent basis, rather than always segregating the weaker readers. The more able and confident children will be good role models to those less capable. As well as this, children in a group share in the successes of the group in general.

✔ Promote success by providing the children with many different ways to access text. Give as much support as is necessary for children who cannot read a text independently, allowing them to participate as equal partners in response activities.

✔ Find opportunities for every child to be an expert at some time. Use your interest profiles for this.

✔ Provide one-to-one help when possible. You can use other children or classroom volunteers for this. Make sure all the children understand the tasks they are to do, know how to get started and have someone to go to for help when they are stuck.

✔ Provide reading partners for children who need help. Train them so they know how to help and keep the partners together over a long period of time, so an atmosphere of trust can develop. Working in pairs can help both children to gain confidence.

✔ Provide listening tapes, so children can listen, read along while listening and then try to read independently. You can make the tapes yourself, or ask another child or parent volunteer. You can build up a library of stories on tape that all the children will enjoy.

✔ Encourage children to respond to reading other than through writing. Children who are reluctant readers are often also insecure writers. Provide a variety of ways to respond: through talk, movement or visual arts.

✔ Do not insist that children finish every book they start. Adults do not continue reading books they find boring; children should have the same choices. At the same time, be aware of the children who are 'reading squirrels', always collecting books but never finishing any of them. Help these children to choose a book that is within their interests and abilities and tell them you will talk about it when they have finished it.

✔ Keep parents informed of each child's successes and progress. Every child should have a growing list of skills and competencies.

✔ Enlist the help of the family to encourage, not criticize, their children and to set aside a time for all the family to read at home. Work with families of beginning readers to demonstrate good practice. Encourage them initially to read to their children. When the child is able, they should take turns to read.

✔ Suggest that parents listen to their children read, but do not look at the page at the same time. Looking over the child's shoulder creates an evaluative situation, where word accuracy is being checked. Instead, just sit and listen, giving the child the freedom to make reasonable predictions and substitutions. Reading time at home can become a social event, rather than a test of reading accuracy.

✔ Above all, self-esteem is linked to success. Limit the tasks and expectations you set sufficiently, so that your reluctant readers can feel successful most of the time.

Making reading interesting

Have a wide range of reading materials that will meet a variety of interests and needs. Use some of these as basic reading material, as well as having them available for recreational reading.

Less able children particularly may benefit from the use of technology. Basic phonic and spelling practice is often more attractive to them when played as games on a computer. A typewriter or word-processor keyboard may also help them to put some of their own plots into print.

Although computers are becoming much more familiar in classrooms, it is easy to forget more inexpensive resources such as the cassette recorder, which can be used to listen to text read aloud, to rehearse or practise oral reading and to plan writing.

It would be a fallacy to suggest that reading is easier on the Internet or on screen, but it has the tremendous advantage of providing in-built motivation. Many children who find reading a struggle may also be less likely to use all the facilities of a PC at home, and therefore you need to make sure that they have ample opportunity to use them in school.

Possible reading materials

- ✔ Fiction and non-fiction.
- ✔ Stories.
- ✔ 'How to' books.
- ✔ Technical magazines.
- ✔ Sports magazines.
- ✔ Biographies.
- ✔ Newspapers.
- ✔ Catalogues.
- ✔ Posters.
- ✔ Advertisements.
- ✔ Child-written stories and reports.

Keep an interest profile for each child. Use this to help you to choose materials for the classroom library, stories to read aloud and themes for projects. You will also be aware of who knows about specific subject areas, such as stamp collecting, horse riding or speaking Portuguese, and so will be able to call on those children as experts.

Provide time for children to read books of their own choice. Do not be critical or disapproving if children choose comic books, picture books or books you think too short or too easy; children will not typically spend long with books they find too easy.

Do not always follow up a reading task with activities. Sometimes, ask the children simply to read for fun.

Read aloud every day, even if it is just a joke or a clip from the local newspaper. Show children that print contains fun, information and entertainment.

Set tasks that make reading necessary. This could be cooking from a recipe, assembling a model from instructions, learning a game using the rulebook, or filling in an application form. Post signs in the classroom; write a daily joke on the board. Activities such as these will demonstrate to reluctant readers that reading is part of everyday life and is hard to get along without.

Use your growing repertoire of ways to read and respond to reading. Vary the activities children do before, during and after reading. The more variety there is, the more stimulating your reading period will be.

Broaden the children's knowledge and tastes by introducing new books, doing book talks, reading short passages out loud and visiting the school library. Provide time for other children to recommend books, either by conducting a book talk or by writing a short review for the noticeboard.

Older non-readers

Children who have fallen behind their peers in reading will have difficulty in every school subject. It is important to deal with their reading difficulties, while at the same time giving them all the help they need in content area subjects. These children need a two-fold strategy:

1. Extra help to improve reading.
2. Assistance with getting by in other subjects in the meantime.

Because much of the text for beginning readers will be too childish for them, the language experience approach may work well. They can dictate their 'stories', perhaps personal experiences or opinions, before reading them back.

Assisting older non-readers

✔ Help the children to develop their writing. Encourage them to spell phonetically, just as beginning spellers do. Writing and spelling are excellent ways for people of any age to learn how words are constructed and how to decode them.

✔ Provide help with the reading they need to do in other subjects.

✔ Provide a reading partner to work with the child in class. If necessary, the partner can read everything aloud.

✔ Find a volunteer to tape-record any readings the child needs to do, whether in history or mathematics. This would be good practice for another child in rehearsed oral reading.

✔ Enlist a volunteer in the family to do the reading necessary for homework.

✔ With sufficient help, the children may be able to upgrade reading skills while maintaining a level of success in other subjects.

Reproducibles

Student reproducibles

Reading Log
Ask children to keep a record of books they have read. Encourage children to comment on each book. Comments can be personal reflections, or refer to response activities the children have been involved in. If children are willing to share their reading logs, post them in the classroom library so other children can see which books their classmates have read.

Books I Have Read
Ask students to keep a record of their reading, and to help rate books according to level of reading difficulty. You can use this information in a guided reading program to help children progress through texts of increasing difficulty.

Graph Your Reading
Children can use this chart to keep records of the kinds of books they read. This is a great way to expand the children's range of reading and make them aware of different topics and genres. You can do this through themes, book talks and special classroom displays. You can also link this with instruction on how the library is organized.

My Reading
To become independent readers, and take control of their learning, children need to be aware of their own strengths and weaknesses. You can use this reproducible as a guide for talking to children about their reading, as topics for group discussion, or as a questionnaire. Choose three or four statements to focus on at a time to build up a record of what students feel about their own reading.

About My Reading
Diagnosing attitude is often a first step in identifying reading problems. You can use questions like these as a guide for talking to students, as topics for group discussion or as a questionnaire.

Storyboard Template
Children can use this storyboard template as a way to examine story structure, or to plan or retell a story.

Book Review
Here are two templates for children to use to review their reading, one for young children, and one for older students. You can make book reviews voluntary, as a way to encourage critical reading. Make the completed reviews available for others to read, either by posting them on the bulletin board, or by setting up a binder in the classroom library.

Teacher reproducibles

Responding Opportunities
You can use some or all of these categories as a guide for planning activities to follow reading. For specific teaching suggestions in each category, see Chapter 5. The activities you plan will also provide subject matter and context for your talking and writing program.

Prompts for Assisted Retelling
You can use these headings to help you plan discussion and/or activities following a reading experience. Asking questions can help children reflect on their reading, and prompt deeper thought and comprehension. It is not necessary to use all the sections for every reading session. The kind of text will indicate which is appropriate.

Evaluation Summary
Because reading involves so many different kinds of skill and knowledge, averages are not useful when deciding what help students need. Records need to show in detail what each student can and cannot do. You can use this chart periodically during the year, and comment on the student's competence in each category. You will find this detailed record useful when reporting to parents, discussing growth and progress with the child or writing reports.

Program Assessment
Use this checklist periodically during the year to monitor the reading and teaching experiences you are providing, and to assess how complete your reading program is. Reviewing this chart from time to time during the year can help you plan future reading and response activities.

Sharing In Your Child's Reading Progress
A parent's guide to helping at home
To support reading at home, share these guidelines with parents at the beginning of the school year or during parent-teacher interviews.

Developing Comprehension (see p. 79) and *Teaching and Learning for Literacy* (see p. 79) illustrate the key principles from which the ideas, strategies and activities in this book are based. You can use this information for context, reference and as a guideline for planning your own reading programs.

Reading Log

Name _____

Date	Title & author	Comments

Books I Have Read

Name _____

Rate your books: Easy = E;   Difficult but readable = M;   Very difficult = D

Title	Author	Finished yes or no	Rating

Graph Your Reading

Name _____

Date started _____ Date finished _____

Starting on the left, color in a box for each kind of book or story you read.
Add any other categories you need.

Humor																							
Mystery																							
Fantasy																							
Fairy tale																							
Sports																							
Nature																							
Science fiction																							
Detective																							
Adventure																							
Biography																							
Autobiography																							
Mythology																							
Romance																							
Poetry																							
How to																							
Comic strip																							
Newspaper																							
Magazine																							

My Reading

Name _____   Date _____

The most interesting thing I have read recently is

_____

_____

I found it interesting because

_____

_____

The most difficult thing I have read recently is

_____

_____

It was difficult because

_____

_____

Ways my reading has improved:

_____

_____

How I improved these things:

_____

_____

Things that cause me problems when I read:

_____

_____

How I might solve these problems:

_____

_____

About My Reading

Name _____   Date _____

Are you a good reader?

_____

How do you know?

_____

_____

Do you like to read? Explain.

_____

_____

What do you read at home?

_____

_____

What kinds of reading in school do you like?

_____

_____

Are there kinds of reading in school you do not like?

_____

Explain.

_____

_____

How do you feel when you are asked to read aloud?

_____

_____

If you were going to help someone become a better reader, what would you
teach them to do?

_____

_____

Storyboard Template

Name _____

In each box, draw an event from a story. This can be a story you have read or your own story. Beside each box describe the drawing in words.

Book Review

Reviewer's name _____

Title of book _____

Author & illustrator _____

What the story was about

_____

_____

_____

_____

What I think about this book

_____

_____

_____

_____

_____

Book Review

Reviewer's name _____

Title of book _____

Author & illustrator _____

Synopsis

_____

_____

_____

_____

Review

_____

_____

_____

_____

_____

Responding Opportunities

Reading Text/theme _____

Reflecting	Talking	Writing
Related reading	Drama	Other media

Prompts for Assisted Retelling

Text _____

1. Setting

2. Characters

3. Problems/conflicts

4. Events

5. Resolution

6. Personal reactions/response

Evaluation Summary

Name _____   Date _____

Attitude/confidence	
Quantity of reading	
Range of reading	
Use of the reading process	
Levels of comprehension – narrative	
Level of comprehension – expository	
Reference skills	
Other	

Program Assessment

Do the students:	Date	Comments
Read daily? – teacher-selected material – self-selected material – in different subject areas		
Read different kinds of text? – novels – short stories – picture books – poetry – cartoons – songs – non-fiction – reference – environmental print — signs, labels – visual media		
Read in different modes? – silent – choral – oral – dramatic		
Use reading for different purposes? – for enjoyment – to entertain others – for information – to follow instructions		
Work in different groupings? – whole class – pairs – mixed-ability group – ability group – special-interest group – independent		
Reflect and respond in a variety of ways? – independent thought – discussion – written responses – drama/role-playing – teacher and peer conferences – representing through different media		

Sharing in Your Child's Reading
A parent's guide to helping at home

- Show that you value reading in your family.
  - Let your child see you reading, for pleasure and for information.
  - Talk about what you like to read.
  - Visit the public library. Take out books yourself.
  - Give books as gifts.
  - Use reading for real purposes: lists, memos, notes, letters, and Yellow Pages.
- Read aloud to your child regularly.
  - Read stories chosen by your child.
  - Read novels chapter by chapter as a serial.
  - Ask your librarian for suggestions on quality children's literature.
  - Use picture books, even with older children.
- Read Together.
  - Cook together using a recipe.
  - Share interesting stories from the newspaper.
  - Check the sports results on the Internet or in the newspaper.
  - Choose programs from TV listings.
  - Read the mail: letters, e-mail, flyers, notices and bills.
- Accentuate the positive.
  - Try to respond to what your child does right. Your child will build on strengths, not on weaknesses.
  - Your child will learn in small steps, not giant leaps. Look for and reward small achievements.
- Give your child real-life reading and writing jobs.
  - Follow the map when you go on a journey.
  - Read bus and train schedules.
  - Find numbers in the telephone book.
  - Jot down phone messages.
  - Make the shopping list.
  - Send postcards and greeting cards.
- Encourage your child to read to you.
  - Be a friendly audience, not a judge. Regard reading as a sharing experience, not a test.
  - When your child reads aloud, do not look over his or her shoulder. This creates a test situation and can cause anxiety.
  - Do not correct misread words. Just ask your child to re-read a sentence if it does not make sense.
  - Talk about the meaning of the text, not the mistakes your child has made.
- Make sure your child looks forward to future reading experiences at home.
  - Praise success.
  - Give what help is needed in a supportive way.
  - Judge how much your child can manage without becoming frustrated, bored or tired. Little and often is a good rule.

Developing Comprehension

Comprehension is a many-layered cognitive activity. It takes place before, during and after reading. We can teach children how to reflect and respond to reading. Different kinds of text require different kinds of thinking, so our approach must be as varied as possible.

On different levels
Literal
Inferential
Critical
Creative

At different times
Before reading
During reading
After reading

In different ways
Reflect
Talk
Write
Read/find out
Dramatize
Model

In different groupings

Whole class
Small group
Pairs
Individual

Ability
Mixed ability
Interest
Friendship

Teaching and Learning for Literacy

Success in reading and writing involves understanding and integrating all aspects of language.

Process
Knowing how to go about the tasks of reading and writing.
Thinking the way fluent readers think.
Working with writing as a drafting process.

Meaning
Knowing that understanding or conveying meaning is the primary task.
Making meaning the main focus of a reading task.
Focusing on meaning in first-draft writing.
Using meaning to make spelling links.

Style
Recognizing the many different purposes for written language.
Working in different modes and genres of written text.
Recognizing different expressive, transactional and poetic modes of language.

Organization
Organizing information so it can be accessed at a future time.
Understanding sequencing, paragraphing and organizational formats.
Reading texts written in different formats.

Grammar
Using and understanding standard forms of grammar and syntax.
Using syntactic information to predict while reading.

Spelling
Understanding how letters are used and grouped to represent sounds (phonics).
Understanding spelling as a word-building process.
Using word-building knowledge to encode and decode text.

Punctuation
Using punctuation as an aid to reading.
Using punctuation to support meaning in writing.

Index